Sobbing Superpower

SELECTED POEMS OF TADEUSZ RÓŻEWICZ

Translated from the Polish by

JOANNA TRZECIAK

Foreword by

EDWARD HIRSCH

W. W. NORTON & COMPANY · NEW YORK · LONDON

For information about permission to reproduce selections from this book,
write to Permissions, W. W. Norton & Company, Inc.,
500 Fifth Avenue, New York, NY 10110

For information about special discounts for bulk purchases,
please contact W. W. Norton Special Sales at
specialsales@wwnorton.com or 800-233-4830

Manufacturing by Courier Westford
Book design by JAMdesign
Production manager: Anna Oler

Library of Congress Cataloging-in-Publication Data

Różewicz, Tadeusz.
[Poems. English. Selections]
Sobbing superpower : selected poems of Tadeusz Rozewicz / [Tadeusz Różewicz] ;
translated from the Polish by Joanna Trzeciak ; foreword by Edward Hirsch.
p. cm.
ISBN 978-0-393-06779-8
1. Różewicz, Tadeusz—Translations into English.
I. Trzeciak, Joanna. II. Hirsch, Edward. III. Title.
PG7158.R63A2 2011
891.8'517—dc22
2010045343

W. W. Norton & Company, Inc.
500 Fifth Avenue, New York, N.Y. 10110
www.wwnorton.com

W. W. Norton & Company Ltd.
Castle House, 75/76 Wells Street, London W1T 3QT

1 2 3 4 5 6 7 8 9 0

To John and Imre Huss

Contents

From *On the Surface and Inside a Poem*
(Na powierzchni poematu i w środku), **1983**

From *Bas-Relief (Płaskorzeźba)*, **1991**

From *always a fragment (zawsze fragment)*, **1996**

From *always a fragment. recycling (zawsze fragment. recycling)*, **1998**

From *the professor's knife (nożyk profesora)*, **2001**

From Jan Różewicz, *Mercutio's Cards (Karty merkucja)*, 1998

From an unpublished manuscript, 2008

Acknowledgments

Poems in this book have appeared in the following publications:

New Ohio Review: "In the Light of Day," "My Lips"

Field Magazine: "Homework Assignment on the Subject of Angels"

My Favorite Poem Project: "Posthumous Exoneration"

Tri-Quarterly: "the professor's knife," "But Whoever Sees . . . ," " * * * (I waded through the dream)," "The Wall," "Chestnut Tree," "Photograph," " * * * (At dawn the light)," "The Boat," "Return to the Forest"

One Hundred Great Poems of the Twentieth Century, ed. Mark Strand: "In the Middle of Life"

Words without Borders: "Trains" (part I of "the professor's knife")

Tin House: "Francis Bacon or Diego Velázquez in the dentist's chair"

Virginia Quarterly Review: "Survivor," "The Story of Old Women," "Autumnal," "As You're Leaving," "My Poetry," "a finger to the lips," "Butcher's Booths"

Sobbing Superpower

Foreword

Tadeusz Różewicz is a poet of dark refusals, hard negations. He is a naked or impure poet ("I crystallize impure poetry," he writes), an antipoet relentlessly, even ruthlessly determined to tell the truth, however painful it may be. He scorns the idea of the poet as prophet and speaks from the margins—a stubborn outsider. "A poet is one who believes / and one who cannot," he declares. He dwells in uncertainties and doubts, in the insecure, gray areas of life—skepticism is his native mindset—and strips poetry down to its bare essentials: words alone on a page. He is bracingly clear and shuns the floridities—the grand consolations—of the traditional lyric. His characteristic free-verse style is a nonstyle, a zero-sum game. "I have no time for aesthetic values," he says. Rather, he treats modern poetry as "a battle for breath" and writes with an anxious, prolific, offhanded urgency. He is wary and intense, a bemused seer of nothingness. I consider him the Samuel Beckett of modern Polish poetry.

Różewicz belongs to a brilliant generation of Polish poets—the half generation after Czesław Miłosz—initiated in the apocalyptic fires of history. He is a crucial part of the firmament—the "Generation of Columbuses"—that includes such other great modern poets as Zbigniew Herbert and Wisława Szymborska. He grew up during one of the few periods of independence in Polish history, but came of age during the terrible years of World War II. Poland lost six million people during the war, nearly one fifth of its population, and all young writers felt the crushing burden of speaking for those who did not survive the German occupation. "I'm twenty-four / Led to slaughter / I survived," Różewicz wrote in "Survivor" (*Anxiety,* 1947). It was no boast. For him, poetry—or at least one kind of poetry—was murdered during the war. The Holocaust loomed over everything.

The war was such a traumatic event that for a new generation of Polish poets it called all moral and aesthetic values into question. Those who survived could never believe in the future again. Nor could they revert to traditional forms of poetry. They rejected the aesthetics of elaborate, ornamental, or sonorous language. No more intricate meters and rhymes, no more fancy metaphors. It was as if poetry had to be reinvented from the ground up. Różewicz fostered this distrust of rhetoric, of false words and sentiments. He was among the first to catch the mood in a stripped-down poetry of drastic simplicity. Here is the beginning of "In the Middle of Life," which reads like a new kind of primer:

> After the end of the world
> after my death
> I found myself in the middle of life
> creating myself
> building a life
> people animals landscapes
>
> this is a table I kept saying
> this is a table
> on the table are bread knife
> the knife is used for cutting bread
> people feed on bread
>
> man should be loved
> I learned by night by day
> what should one love
> I answered man

Różewicz's brutal simplicity enacts his suspicion of all general ideas and philosophies. He distrusts overarching concepts ("Concepts are only words"). He had a moment of embracing Communism, but soon gave it up, and over the years he has shown himself to be temperamentally allergic to political creeds or ideologies, public speech, sobbing superpowers from the East or West. He is alert to official lies and recognizes that evil comes "from a human being / always a human being / and only a human being." His clear-eyed view of humanity is one of the constants of his work. "It would be best to go insane / you're right Tadeusz," he writes to his friend Tadeusz Konwicki, "but our generation never quite goes insane / we keep our eyes open / to the very end."

What an abiding pleasure it is to read Joanna Trzeciak's precise and insightful translation of Różewicz's poetry. She captures his cunning style of negation, his stark diction and sudden turns, his talkativeness, his well-timed silences, his artful artlessness. For more than sixty years, Tadeusz Różewicz has remained utterly true to his values and commitments, to his dark view that "nothing begets nothing." He is spare and uncompromising, a magician without robes. "My poetry," he writes, "justifies nothing / explains nothing / renounces nothing / encompasses no whole / fulfills no hope." And yet: "it obeys its own imperative / its own capabilities / and limitations / it loses against itself." In the end, Różewicz's unlikely creativity—the life force itself—has always won out. He inveighs against singing, but sings nonetheless. He can't go on, he will go on. "A poet is one who exits / and one who cannot," he concludes. He has given us an unwavering and undefended poetry, a self-contradictory poetry that attacks mankind but defends individual men. So, too, over the decades, the poet of negativity has been slowly, cautiously, and firmly building "a bridge / linking the past / to the future." He has created the poetry of qualified humanism. He rescues consciousness from oblivion. As he writes in "so what it's a dream":

> I write on water
>
> from a few sentences
> from a few verses
> I build an arc
>
> to save something
> from the flood
> that catches us by surprise

—EDWARD HIRSCH

Translator's Note

Simply one of the great witnesses to the twentieth century, Różewicz gives voice in a sharp, disturbing, and clear way to the crisis of values that has plagued our civilization—the impotence of culture, science, and religion when confronted with unspeakable evil. He has always been drawn to risk and reinvention, and his transformative effect on poetics has been felt by all the poets of his generation, Wisława Szymborska and Czesław Miłosz included. In the twenty-first century he continues to leave his mark, influencing yet another generation of Polish poets. Now in his late eighties, the poet emeritus, as he calls himself, remains prolific, having published four collections of poems since I undertook the project in 2002. This is not counting his *Collected Works* (*Utwory zebrane: Poezja,* 2005–2006), where he has reworked many of his earlier poems, the revisions part of an ongoing dialogue with his readership. Różewicz's poetry is rife with conversations, some with the greats of the century—Bacon, Pound, Beckett, Wittgenstein, Heidegger, Celan—others with his intimates—mother, father, brother, wife, close friends. The volume ends in a call and response between son and father: a poem by Różewicz's son Jan (1953–2008) and Różewicz's heretofore unpublished reply. Herein I have chosen poems from throughout the entire span of Różewicz's long (and ongoing) poetic career. My selections are weighted heavily toward the poet's earliest and most recent collections, with poems plucked from the intervening period to sketch the contours of his stylistic and thematic experimentation in the hope that the present volume might give a sense of the arc of Różewicz's verse. Trying to represent his prolific output in a volume of selected works is like trying to sample the ocean with a sieve, but I have tried.

Różewicz's poetry offers myriad challenges to the translator. His "poetry after Auschwitz," wherein values, ideals, and even language had to be reinvented, is an antipoetry: minimalist, powerful, and raw. His innovation was to reject every linguistic element that separated poetry from the naked truth. To convey, in the words of Adam Zagajewski, Różewicz's "supernatural simplicity" has not been simple.

Różewicz's poetic path has been marked by formal experimentation that draws in part upon his prose writing and work in theater and film. In the early 1960s his poetics began to expand to encompass impure form, a welding of literary and nonliterary forms of great diversity and disparity. Fragments of David Sylvester's interviews with the painter Francis Bacon for the BBC, government statistical ledgers on European rates of beef consumption, captions, ads for art exhibitions, transcripts from the trial of Ezra Pound, fragments of Różewicz's own poetry (and that of Dante, Celan, Pound, Eliot, Beckett, and others), theatrical stage directions, fragments of personal correspondence, a neon litany of streetside signs from a swinging neighborhood of postwar Munich—all of these find a place in his poetry. One task of the translator has been to sleuth out these source texts, which are often mediated by German and Polish translations and hence can easily escape detection.

German plays many roles within Różewicz's poetry. As his second language, it afforded him access to information from the West while living under the Communist regime in Poland. It is the language in which some of his most beloved poetry (Goethe, Hölderlin, Celan, Canetti, Benn) and philosophy (Wittgenstein, Nietzsche, Heidegger, Jaspers) is written. German was also the language of the enemy, the occupying power, the language in which the blueprint for the Holocaust was written. During World War II Różewicz monitored German radio and read German newspapers for the Polish resistance. Thus the presence of German words in his poetry has a symbolic significance that still resonates with his Polish readership. Yet that invasive presence would not be felt in the same way by an English reader. So how does one capture in English translation this multivalent role of German? I used a variety of strategies for handling the pervasive presence of German in the text—retaining it untranslated, replacing it with English, or supplementing it with a translation either alongside it or below it—whatever appeared to suit the case at hand. Wherever the German has been replaced by an English translation, italics have been used and the German provided in the notes, along with the rationales for the various strategies pursued.

As a poet engaged with the times in which he has lived, Różewicz inevitably makes a number of cultural references, not all of which will be immediately obvious to even the most erudite Anglophone reader. There are also many allusions to both literary and nonliterary texts, and reference is made to people close to him: friends, family, translators, journalists, artists, art historians, poets, writers, and playwrights. To avoid distraction, I have provided glosses in the notes to individual poems toward the end of the book. In addition to the sources cited, some information in the notes was culled from Zbigniew Majchrowski's biography, *Różewicz* (2002).

This project went through many stages and the list of those who deserve thanks is long and undoubtedly incomplete. My thanks go first and foremost to Tadeusz Różewicz, who entrusted his poetry to a stranger he met in a park, and to Jan Stolarczyk, who set in motion a process that led to this book. I also thank Różewicz for our long conversations over the phone about his poems, and for sharing with me his time, his manuscripts, and his vodka. My heartfelt thanks goes to Wiesława Różewicz nee Kozłowska for her hospitality, and to Kamil Różewicz for conversations about philosophy and roses. Jan Stolarczyk continued to provide guidance all along the way. I owe him my gratitude for the books he furnished me when they were nowhere to be found. Ewa and Cezary Kaszewski, and their sons Piotr and Paweł opened their home to us and filled our stays in Wrocław with great art.

Robert Hass, Mark Strand, W. S. Merwin, Susan Hahn, David Young, and Edward Hirsch provided much support for the project. I owe a debt of gratitude to Susan Hahn for her encouragement, and for her unwavering enthusiasm for Różewicz's poetry. Thanks also to the late Amy Bartlett of *Tin House,* for her insightful editorial suggestions and to Philip Levine for his encouragement early on. Oriana Walker, Liam Singer, and Adonia Lugo assisted me in the early stages of the project. Mark Strand read the entire manuscript and offered his perfect pitch.

Jutta Ittner, Sue Ellen Wright, and Aleksandra von Seckendorff helped with several of the German passages. Jewel Spears Brooker, Tomasz Kunz, Piotr Śliwiński, and Izabela Kalinowska offered scholarly insight and a sounding board, particularly for the notes to the poems. Bożena Shallcross read parts of the manuscript and lent it her analytic prowess and great eye for detail. Samuel Sandler commented on a number of individual poems, Polish originals in hand. For her support during the final phase of the project I would like to thank Ewa Zadrzyńska.

This project was greatly facilitated by fellowships from the National Endowment for the Humanities and the Newhouse Center for the Humanities at Wellesley College, and a grant from the Division of Research and Graduate Studies at Kent State University. Tim Peltason created an ideal environment for intellectual exchange at the Newhouse Center. Brian Baer deserves thanks for holding down the fort during my NEH Fellowship. Thanks go to Greg Shreve and to my generous colleagues in the Institute for Applied Linguistics, the Department of Modern and Classical Language Studies, NEOMFA Program in Creative Writing, and the Wick Poetry Center at Kent State.

Adrienne and Roger Rosenberg have remained a great source of support for me since my Dallas days. My parents, Wiesław and Olga, who raised me in a spirit of appreciation for poetry, have always been there for me, and my gratitude is boundless. Thanks also go to the entire Huss family for bearing with me over various holidays and to the Hoffman and Labby families for their generosity. Danuta Kułyk helped with logistical support and queries. Barbara Domagała brought joy into our lives in the final stages of the project.

Edward Hirsch, tireless champion of Polish poetry, has given his all to the Różewicz cause. I am honored and delighted to have this volume open with his foreword. David Young commented on the entire manuscript and offered numerous suggestions that greatly improved it. My editor at W. W. Norton, Jill Bialosky, has been a steady hand: patient, generous, and supportive.

Finally, none of this would have been possible without the help of my husband John Huss who read and commented on the manuscript in all its stages. Imre Huss slowed things down, and in doing so put me in touch with the pulse of life in ways that poetry alone cannot.

—JOANNA TRZECIAK
Cleveland, September 30, 2009

From

Anxiety,

1947

Rose

Rose is the name of a flower
or a dead girl

You can place a rose in a warm palm
or in black soil

A red rose screams
one with golden hair passed in silence

Blood drains from the pale petal
the girl's dress hangs formless

A gardener tends tenderly to a bush
a father who survived rages in madness

Five years have passed since Your death
flower of love that knows no thorn

Today a rose bloomed in the garden
memory of the living and faith have died.

1945

Mask

I'm watching a film about the Carnival of Venice
where giant puppets
grin silently from ear to ear
and a girl too beautiful for me
a resident of a small northern town
rides astride an ichthyosaur.

Excavations in my country yield small black
heads cruel smiles sealed shut with plaster
but even we have a garish whirling merry-go-round
and a lady in black stockings who coaxes
an elephant two blue lions with red tongues
and catches a wedding ring in mid flight.

Our bodies are unyielding and reluctant to mourn
our palates taste love
let us adjust the paper ribbons and wreaths
crouch down: let hip touch hip
your thighs are alive
let us flee let us flee.

1946

A Crumb

I want to tell her
that our love
is like a tiny
nest
lined with down
and twitter.

Perched on a volcano.

Her hair glows
like feathers of light
happiness whose every crumb
feeds the hungry.

I the fire-eater
from the conflagration
want to tell her
with charred cracked lips

But in the palm of her hand she holds
just one crumb
she rescued and carried
running
through fire and water.

Lament

I turn to you priests
teachers judges artists
shoemakers physicians public officials
and to you Father
Hear me out

I am not young
let neither my slender body
nor the tender whiteness of my neck
deceive you
nor the brightness of my broad forehead
nor the down above my sweet lip
nor the cherubic laughter
nor the springy step

I am not young
let neither my innocence
nor my purity
move you
nor my weakness
fragility or simplicity

I am twenty
I am a murderer
I am a tool
as blind as a sword
in the hands of an executioner
I've murdered a man

Maimed I saw
neither sky nor rose
nor bird nor nest nor tree
nor Saint Francis
nor Achilles nor Hector
For six years
fumes of blood gushed from my nose
I don't believe in water turned to wine
I don't believe in the forgiveness of sins
I don't believe in the resurrection of the dead

Double Sentence

I see the smile
wiped off his white face
over by the wall

The anonymous harbinger of death
hangs his head
lower

I see
the comical image of grief
in worn-out slippers
over by the stove
the small crooked
figure
of a mother turned
to stone.

To the Dead

My concerns belong to the living.

I see hear touch
weigh myself on a street scale
I dodge a blue tram
In July I wipe the sweat off a shiny forehead
I drink raspberry soda
I am tired
I am bored I write poems
I think about death
I buy pretzels and fuzzy
peaches that look like baby mice
I read Marx
I don't understand Bergson
I go out dancing with a redhead
and we laugh
about the A-bomb
the red circle of lips
a long golden straw
my girl in a green blouse
drinks the moon from the sky
a waiter carries foamy beer around
lights glisten on the eyelashes of evening
the memory of you
covered my anxiety with a hand.

These are my concerns. I live
and nothing is as alien to me
as you my dead Friend.

Survivor

I'm twenty-four
Led to slaughter
I survived.

These words are empty and equivalent:
man and animal
love and hate
foe and friend
dark and light.

Man is killed just like an animal
I've seen:
truckloads of chopped-up people
who will never be saved.

Concepts are only words:
virtue and vice
truth and lie
beauty and ugliness
courage and cowardice.

Virtue and vice weigh the same
I've seen:
a man who was both
vicious and virtuous.

I'm searching for a teacher and a master
let him give me back my sight hearing and speech
let him name objects and concepts again
let him separate the light from the dark.

I'm twenty-four
Led to slaughter
I survived.

The Magician's Apprentice

Why did I open my eyes
Flooded by a world of shape and color
wave upon wave
shape upon shape
hue upon hue
left at the mercy of
venomous greens
cold blues
intense yellow suns
bright red lips
I am insatiable.

Why did I open my ears
living voices filled me
echoes of the voices of the dead
even a tear cuts my face with a screech
like a diamond cutting glass
and silence stretched like the skin
of a war drum thunders
poor wretch I can even hear the grass grow.

Why did I loosen my tongue
forfeiting a telling silence
a gabbler who will say nothing new
under the sun.

Wide open
not knowing the incantation
I cannot
shut myself off.

The Living Were Dying

The walled-in living were dying
black flies laid their eggs
in human flesh.
Soon
the streets were paved
with swollen heads.

Aaron the father
with a beard of mold and moss
and a head of white light
flickering and fading
ate out of a hand
with limp lips
and kept his turquoise eyes open
until he perished.

Bodies swelled
in a small room.

Salcia sold silvery apples
smelling of orchards
at a gate
of sky blue.

Between the gibberish
and reddish spit
between the lichen on the wall
and the corpse of a pedestrian
with a cruel eye
between a stone
and a madman's wail
stood Salcia in a red dress
yet hues were soaking up venom
and apples rotted in hand.

No one carried apples to the ghetto any longer
no one was buying apples there.
Soon
the bodies started to fall.

Of My House

Of my house
stone upon stone
flower on wallpaper
bird and twig

A threshold dividing the emptiness from the rubble
a horseshoe above the threshold

I will not cross that luck
now or ever

walls as open
as the corners of the globe

on one side is the wind
that blew away the smoke and my father

on the other side is the wind
that blew away the smoke and my mother

on the third side is the wind
that blew away even the name of my brother

Parting

She thought
that the world around her
was sad
that flowers and rain were sad
that sorrow had nestled itself
in coarse wool
smelling of reseda
that the voices
of those leaving
were sad
that the jolly carriage driver
cracking the whip
was sad
she thought that
heaven and earth
were sad beyond measure
but
these were just wheels turning
faster and further.

Broad and boundless.

As You're Leaving

At dawn as you're leaving
your contours shucked out of night
a bright violin
your birch hips
bowed
taut strings
still vibrating.

Enveloped encased
by your touch
a cover of caresses
so sweet
I will not drift off into sleep.

Eyelids open wider
are now filled by a day
as bright as the white of an eye
and as pure.

Purification

Don't be ashamed of tears
don't be ashamed of tears young poets.

Be enchanted by the moon
by the moonlit night
pure love and the song of a nightingale.

Don't be afraid of ascension
reach toward a star
compare eyes to stars.

Be moved by primroses
orange butterflies
sunrises and sunsets.

Feed the gentle pigeons corn
observe with a smile
dogs flowers rhinoceroses and locomotives.

Speak of ideals
recite an ode to youth
trust the stranger passing by.

Naïve ones—you will come to believe in beauty
once moved, you will come to believe in a human being.

Don't be ashamed of tears
don't be ashamed of tears young poets.

From

Red Glove,

1948

Chestnut Tree

It's the saddest thing to leave
home on an autumn morning
where nothing forebodes a timely return

The chestnut tree Father planted
in front of the house grows before our eyes

Mother is tiny
you can carry her in your arms

jars stand on the shelf
and the fruit preserves inside them
are like goddesses whose sweet lips
retain the taste
of eternal youth

the army of soldiers in the corner of the drawer
will remain tin till the end of the world

and God almighty who mixed
bitterness into the sweetness
hangs on the wall helpless
and badly painted

Childhood is like the worn-out face
on a gold coin that rings
pure.

The Wall

She turned her face to the wall

but she loves me
why did she turn away

with one motion of the head
you can turn away from a world
where sparrows chirp
and young people walk around
in loud ties

Now she's alone
facing a dead wall
and that's how she'll stay

there she will stay
against the towering wall
gnarled and small
fists clenched

and here I sit
my legs made of stone
not stealing her away from this place
not carrying her off
lighter than a sigh.

Was

already your smile was
just as the Roman Empire was
that boys in uniforms study
in school

I cannot summon
your kind smile
watching over me
older Brother

Older by a youthful death
of three years

When I speak of you I say he was
as if speaking of the visage of
a Stone Age man.

Butcher's Booths

Rosy ideals hang
quartered in butcher's booths

In stores
clowns' masks are sold
gaudy post-mortem casts
made of our faces
we who live
we who survived
staring
into the eye sockets of war.

But Whoever Sees . . .

But whoever sees my mother
in a gray-blue gown in a white hospital
shaking
stiffening
wooden smile
white gums

A believer of fifty years
she now weeps saying
"I don't know . . . I don't know"

her face is one big murky tear
she clasps her yellow hands like a frightened
girl
her lips are blue

but whoever sees my mother
a frightened little animal
with bulging eye

may he

oh I would like to carry her near my heart
and feed her only sweetness.

How Wonderful

How wonderful I can pick
berries in the woods
I thought
there were no woods or berries.

How wonderful I can stretch out
in the shadow of a tree
I thought trees
no longer gave shade.

How wonderful I am with you
my heart is beating fast
I thought human beings
had no heart.

From

Smiles,

Poems from 1945–2000

*   *   *

Here is a man
puffed up by other men
when they are gone
a dummy will remain

they call him Wise
and everything he says
becomes a saying

they append to his present
a grand and colorful past
like a peacock's tail
like a baboon's bottom

they retouch photographs
mount magical montages
clip his ears
affix beard and moustache
bulk up his arms
out of an average man
they make
a giant

and they carry this puffed-up man
on the shoulders of another
he believes in his own existence
and starts to act

1956

The Black Bus

This black bus
is different from a flock of red ones
boiling over like a pot
on a stove

Inside just one passenger
patient and prostrate
in a wooden coat
buttoned down to the last nail
he will get off at the final stop

No one would kill
to board this bus
quite the contrary

So let's paint all buses
black with a white stripe
Their melancholy sight
will incline people to be
more courteous
getting on
and getting off

From

Five Poems,

1950

Pigtail

When all the women
from the transport had their heads shaved
four workers
with brooms made from linden twigs
swept and gathered up the hair

Behind the clean glass
lies the stiff hair of those gassed
in the gas chambers
there are pins and bone combs
in this hair

No light shines through it
no breeze parts it
no hand touches it
nor rain nor lips

In giant chests
clusters the dried-out hair
of those gassed
and an ashen pigtail
with a little ribbon
pulled on at school by
naughty boys

The Auschwitz Museum, 1948

A Reply

"Let man be noble,
Generous and good!"
—*Goethe*

What does poetry demand
of me
Self-sacrifice
seclusion and melancholy
For me to pass through the crowd
as if I were passing through air

If poetry demands
seclusion
self-sacrifice
and despair
reject it
Does love for wife
love for a child
for whom I'm buying
a small outfit
care for a mother
do these human feelings
kill poetry

Then create a new one
which builds
upon commonplace feelings
simple words
Let it subtract from the human
all that is animal or godlike

Do I have to flee
my home at night
when it's stormy
and die
in a small train station where
a conductor in booming voice
calls out the names of unfamiliar towns

I look at smokestacks rising
vertically over the roofs
of my city

in lit-up homes
are people I love
to whom I gave my eyes lips and hands
and from whom I am taking

for every single one of us
cries at night
wanting to touch a human hand

From

Time that Goes,

1951

Return to the Forest

When I close my eyes I hear
A bird's call the creak of pines
The forest's shallow silence
Marred by our laughter

I see the forest where
I picked wild blueberries with you
The body was very agile then
And young like water

We would return home
With purple lips
Bare feet like wings
aglow fleeing in dust

There's home I see Smoke
Creeping patiently through the sky
And Mother at the window
Her hand shielding her eyes

From

Plains,

1954

Plains (part III)

Down Żabia Street
through a Polish city
walks Rose
in white feathers

It's not a costume ball
for a long time the wind will carry
feathers from the beds
of those
departed

Their bodies will not leave impressions
in the grass of May meadows
nor on the waves which shimmer
under the saffron fins of fishes
their bodies will not leave impressions
in the hay
when a black lightning bolt of swallows
flies with a squawk
through an empty barn with dirt floor

Their bodies will not leave impressions
on any bed sheets

Down Żabia Street
through a Polish city
walks Rose
on uneven cobblestones
past houses with blue stars
and boarded-up windows
walks through a temple
where stray cats
have found their lair
She walks amidst the glowing feathers
on this black day
she walks through your cities neutral Swedes
she walks through your homes theaters places of worship

she walks through your villages neutral Swiss
through your clean towns
clean as tears

She passed as clouds pass
across the sky across the earth without a trace

Within me I preserved
her heartbeat
the silence of her eyes
the warmth and hue of her lips
the heft of her insides
her fleeting thighs
in the shadow of love
the shape of her head
and the reddish dusk of her falling hair
and the small sun of her smile
She passed as clouds pass
but from where is this immeasurably long shadow
being cast

From

Silver Grain,

1955

My Lips

The day is ending
it ends with supper
the brushing of teeth
a kiss
putting things away

so goes one day
a most precious day
that will never return

what did it bring

It passed and went by
morning till night
just like the previous one

My day my
one and only
what have I gotten done
what have I gotten done

Yet maybe this is as it should be
leaving in the morning
returning in the afternoon
repeating a few motions
putting things in order

My day
world's most beautiful diamond
a house of gold
a blue whale
tear in my eye

My thoughts not quite clear
as I stand hands in my pockets
and look through gray streaks of rain
at a maple turning gold

My lips
which told
the truth which lied
which repeated stated
contradicted begged
shouted whispered
cried laughed

My lips
taking shape
around countless
spoken words

Love 1944

Naked defenseless
lips upon lips
eyes
open wide

listening closely

we swam
across a sea
of tears and blood

1954

Father

He walks through my heart
my old father
His whole life he never saved
he never set aside
penny after penny
never bought a home
nor a gold watch
the piggy bank sat empty

He lived like a bird
in song
from one day to the next
but
tell me how a minor civil servant
can live that way
for years

He walks through my heart
my father
in an old hat
he whistles
a cheerful tune
unshaken in his belief
that he will go to heaven

1954

Old Jewish Cemetery at Lesko

Beneath the tires
of wartime trucks
cemeteries
lie flattened
like a long country road

there
the earth's gentle sighs
the Słone Mountains
quietly
float off into the sky

here
beneath the clouds
beneath the crowns of oaks
burrowed into the ground
bristling
with a black stubble
of tombstones
lies the Jewish cemetery

saved
from the pogrom of graves
beneath the clouds
which pass
and shimmer in silence

beneath the green crowns
of oaks
mourned by rain
it falls into time
into silence

1954

From

An Open Poem,

1956

An Open Poem

A BOW

A whip drawn from the night
as if from a sheath

I suffer the drives of animals
with eyes closed
impelled by the beating of blood
driven like a herd
stampeded

my body opens up

animals jump out
mutely sniff the night

the spine of my first lover
bending like a golden bow
in the darkness
drawn taut it freezes

SECOND RECOLLECTION

Autumn

Stood in the window
with cold blue eyes
red fingernails
hands covered
in yellow bile

Your little white hat
blown off by the wind
glides away
rolls down a path
lined by blackthorns
you chase it
laughing and shouting.

You run and run
I catch you in my arms

WHAT WAS HIDDEN

What was hidden
is exposed
we entered each other
as one enters
earth air
fire water
our bodies were trembling
our eyes were closed

As you slept
in the warm belly of the night
rolled into a ball
lips cooled off
I said to my heart:
"hush hush, silly one
no need to leap out

he will remain here
forever
he will not wake up"

VOICES

They wound and torture each other
with silence and words
as if another life
lay ahead of them

they act
as if they had forgotten
that their bodies
are prone to death
that what's inside
is easily destroyed

ruthless toward each other
they are weaker

than plants or animals
a word a smile
a look can kill them

Golden Mountains

The first time
I saw
mountains
I was twenty-six

I did not laugh
or shout
in their presence
I whispered

When I returned home
I wanted to tell
Mother
what mountains were like

It was hard
at night
everything looks different
mountains and words

Mother was silent
perhaps she was tired
and fell asleep

In the clouds
waxed the moon
golden mountain
of the poor

Leave Us Alone

Forget about us
about our generation
live like human beings
forget about us

we envy
the plants and rocks
we envy the dogs

I would like to be a rat
I used to tell her

I would like not to be
I would like to sleep
and wake up after the war
she would say with her eyes closed

forget about us
don't ask us about our youth
leave us alone

In the Middle of Life

After the end of the world
after my death
I found myself in the middle of life
creating myself
building a life
people animals landscapes

this is a table I kept saying
this is a table
on the table are bread knife
the knife is used for cutting bread
people feed on bread

man should be loved
I learned by night by day
what should one love
I answered man

this is a window I kept saying
this is a window
beyond the window is a garden
in the garden I see an apple tree
the apple tree blossoms
the blossoms fall off
fruit forms
ripens

my father picks an apple
the man picking the apple
is my father

I was sitting on the front steps of the house
that old woman
pulling a goat on a rope
is more needed
is worth more

than the seven wonders of the world
anyone who thinks or feels
she isn't needed
is guilty of genocide

this is a man
this is a tree this is bread

people eat to live
I kept repeating to myself
human life is important
human life has great importance
the value of life
exceeds the value of every object
man has made
man is a great treasure
I kept repeating stubbornly

this is water I kept saying
stroking the waves with my hand
talking to the river
water I said
kind water
it is I

the man talked to the water
talked to the moon
to the flowers to the rain
he talked to the earth
to the birds
to the sky

the sky was silent
the earth was silent
if he heard a voice
flowing
from the earth the water the sky
it was the voice of another man

1955

Posthumous Exoneration

The dead
recall our indifference
the dead
recall our silence
the dead
recall our words

The dead see our smiles
stretching from ear to ear
the dead see our bodies
rubbing against each other
the dead hear our lips
smacking

The dead read our books
listen to our speeches
delivered so long ago
the dead study our essays
take part in discussions
already closed
the dead see our hands
converging in applause

The dead see stadiums
choirs bands chanting

all of the living are guilty
guilty are the small children
bearing flowers
guilty are the lovers
guilty are

those who fled are guilty
and those who stayed
those who said yes

and those who said no
those who said nothing

The dead are reckoning the living
the dead will not exonerate us

From

Forms,

1958

Forms

These forms once so well bred
obedient always ready to receive
dead poetic matter
frightened by fire
broke ranks and dispersed

they fling themselves at their creator
tear him up and drag him
down the long streets
which every band school and church procession
has long since marched

meat still breathing
filled with blood
nourishes
these perfect forms

they press so tightly around their prey
that even the silence does not seep
out

December 1956

I Lack Courage

This world so foreign
is an object found at night
my life is unremarkable
out of this life
however
I crystallize impure poetry

A bespectacled critic smiles
I cannot
explain it to him
he must solve the riddle
himself

A week has seven days
on Saturday night
the doors open
and I lack the courage to leave

these paper feelings
the shuffling of dirty cards

At ten at night
death came and said
do not write these words
sit up straight
put down the pen
drop your hands

April 1958

Outstretched

His arms were thrown open
outstretched so broadly so far apart,
that the left hand touched the leafless tree on the horizon
the right one small and clenched into a fist
was hidden in his mother's hand
The head had the shape
of a long black case
from which the violin had been removed
The teeth were set vertically
between ear and eye

This pyramid with a clump of hair on top
lay in the transparent

innards of January
pink and blue

His brother who came out
of the same mother
and left Europe before the war broke out
is now on the other side
of the ocean
smoking a pipe

1957

Dismantled

All memories images feelings facts
concepts experiences combining within me
do not connect do not comprise a whole
within me
only sometimes do they flow up to me to the shore
of my memory touch my skin
gently with dulled claws
I will not lie
I don't comprise a whole I've been broken and dismantled
who will stoop over and take an interest in these fragments
I myself am very busy
who could recall the form of my interior
in this confusion this feverish commotion
in a hallway where a thousand doors open and close
who will re-create the form which
left its imprint neither in white chalk
nor in black charcoal
when abruptly asked
I myself cannot recall it

and they say of me that I am alive

August 1956

The Tower

The body she wears
the one she lays on the bed when tired
the one that has been probed by metal instruments
the body that sadly shakes like a tiny dog
under a sky too large
that joyous body that danced so lightly
had lips and precious eyes
that talked

the skin the sun wandered over
that shed rain
that silence of the skin so ceremonious
stretching above us like a tent

That body I never had
as it belonged only to itself
wanders around a far-off city
sits on a bench resting
indifferent to our
wants
closed off

do not throw that body from the tall tower
do not cut its veins
do not hang it from a rope
do not paint it black or blue

It returns without taking a breath
to its greater mother
earth

Summer 1956

The Door

The masons had gone
leaving a vertical opening in the wall
Sometimes I think
my apartment is too provisional
easily entered
by strangers

If they hadn't left
that opening
I would be a hermit

alas
a revolving door was recently installed
now I spend my time
entering and exiting

through this doorway
enter the matters of this world
a blossoming apple tree
or a small pony
with dewy eyes
has never stood in it
nor a star
a golden beehive
a stream full of fish
or a forget-me-not

and yet I will not brick up this doorway
maybe a good man
will stand in it
and tell me who I am

In a Hurry

He was reading a book
it was Sunday afternoon
in a little known town
in Central Europe

in a prison cell
two people
convicted for their innocence
awaited their sentence

somewhere far away a train rumbled
it was light in the room
it could have been one in the afternoon
he felt
that he had to decide
that he had to do something
right away
after all he had waited twenty years
he knew that he would have to choose
that this was his last chance
he wanted to get up

but he could not recall
what he wanted
his forgetting
was deepening
others near him moved fast
being born and dying in a hurry

December 1956

Letter to the Cannibals

Dear Cannibals
do not look askance
at a man
asking on the train
if a seat is taken

try to understand
other people also have
two legs and a behind

Dear Cannibals
hold on
don't trample the weak
don't gnash your teeth

try to understand
there are many people there will be
many more so make room
give way

Dear Cannibals
do not buy up
all the shoelaces and spaghetti
Do not say with your backs turned:
I me my mine
my stomach my hair
my bunions my pants
my wife my children
my opinion

Dear Cannibals
let's not eat each other Okay?
for we will not be resurrected
Really

1957

From

Conversation with the Prince,

1961

The Return

Among my works there are those
with which I cannot make peace
years pass
I cannot make peace with them
and yet I cannot disown them
they are bad but they are mine
I brought them to life
they live far away from me
indifferent dead
but the time will come when they will all
run up to me
successful and failed
lame and perfect
ridiculed and rejected

and will gather into one

Fear

Your fear is grand
metaphysical
mine is a little bureaucrat
with a briefcase

with a file folder
with a survey
when was I born
what's my livelihood
what have I not done
in what do I lack faith

what am I doing here
when will I stop pretending
where am I going
next

New Comparisons

To what will you compare
day
to night?
to what will you compare
an apple
to a kingdom?
to what will you compare
a body
at night
a silence
between the lips
between
to what will you compare
an eye
a hand in the darkness
the right to the left
teeth tongue lips
a kiss
to what will you compare
a hip
hair
fingers
breath
silence
poetry
in the light of day
at night

From

Green Rose,

1961

Green Rose

"... she embroidered the rose petals in green."
—*Adam Mickiewicz*

I.

Large cities
grow
overpopulated
they depopulate
the wave ebbs
and flows
shoals of people
so close together
one by the next
that the decay is discernible
from the fragments of words
scattered
here and there
one can imagine the interior
but in a swarm
without a queen
we start to live more and more alone
the distance from and to a human being
grows beneath the neon lights
in overpopulated cities
brushing against one another till blood is drawn
we live as if on an island
inhabited by few creatures
we stay with the handful of those closest to us
but even they depart
each off in their own direction
taking with them
vacuum cleaners second-rate art
women children
motorcycles refrigerators
limited stores of information
ashes pseudonyms

a leftover sense of aesthetics
of faith
something more or less like god
something more or less like love
still others
depart for their caves
meat between their teeth
the weaker ones remain
at bars tables
weaker still are those
who support themselves on the shadows of words
but these words are so transparent
that through them one can see death
nothingness
we depart
lingering shutting ourselves off
no one admitting that they are departing
best not create a panic
hence no one ever dies

remember
we have been open
during the times of greatest oppression
other people's suffering and joy
easily reached inside us
your lives rushed in at me
from all sides
now we are covered in armor
and can only see
through cracks
in faces

II.

Inside me
there is something
No I cannot
describe it
there is something inside me

something that was not there
that grows
not grows
but rises up the throat No
wells up motionless
fills me up No
I do not know precisely
it is good that I forget
but what is it
say it straight
is it love
no it is not fear
is it hate
an idea how empty
no it is not an idea
it is nearly everywhere
is it stealing near you
is it moving in plain view
is it silent is it articulate
is it shouting far away
oh yes it is still far away
yes yes
it is still very far away
tell me is it true
that it is still very far
but what is it tell me what
it is already in me
here and there
and elsewhere
but it was not in me
I know it was not
I know it was not
but now it is already in you
rises up your throat
do you feel anything
tell me quickly
how it is inside you
black or white
blind or sun
mute or crying

you say nothing
tell me that it's far away
You don't
say you will run away
you don't say anything
tell me
you cannot speak
no I am not afraid because I never
saw it
maybe we will move away
sure right away
to another place
you will see that everything
will turn out fine No
you say that there is no other
place that we cannot move
you say nothing
I say nothing lies within us

1959–1960

In the Light of Day

Still others
are sitting in the dark
comfortably
candy in mouth
awaiting
a drama or comedy

against a white sheet
women with eyes
that open and close
mouths
swarming with fake teeth
take off their clothes
in front of the crowd

laughter flows
from open bodies
framed by music
and dialogue

here everything is
funny shocking
more engaging
more beautiful
than in the real world
suddenly shrunken
devoid of flavor

When the hero chokes
the heroine
or covers her
in kisses
the audience stops sucking
on its candy
sits with mouths wide open
faces turned
toward a white sheet
emitting
a phosphorescent glow

In the light of day
a real tear
is small and colorless
a real woman
walking past a wall
crying
looks ugly
her nose is red
her eyelashes colorless
stuck together
a stocking on her left leg
twisted around

Lifting Off the Weight

He came to you
and said

you are responsible
neither for the world nor for the end of the world
you have been unburdened
you are like birds and children
play on

and you did

you keep forgetting
that modern poetry
is a battle for breath

1959

I Was Writing

I was writing
for a short while or an hour
evening night
seized by anger
I either trembled or was sitting speechless
beside myself
eyes misting over with tears
I had been writing for a long time
then I noticed
there was no pen in my hand

From

Nothing in Prospero's Robes,

1963

Nothing in Prospero's Robes

Taught human speech
Caliban the slave
awaits

mug in dung
feet in paradise
he sniffs a human
awaits

nothing arrives
nothing in magic robes
Prospero's robes
nothing from streets and lips
from pulpits and towers
nothing from loudspeakers
speaks to nothing
about nothing

nothing begets nothing
nothing brings up nothing
nothing awaits nothing
nothing threatens
nothing sentences
nothing pardons

1962

From

Third Face,

1968

From a Biographical Note

year of birth
place of birth
1921 Radomsko

yes
my biographical note is written
on a page
from my son's notebook
there is still some space left
still a few blank lines

I have crossed out only two sentences
and added one
in a little while
I will toss in a few more words

you ask me for
the more important
events and dates of my life
ask others about it

my biography has neared its end
several times already
at times for the better
at times for the worse

1965

* * *

At dawn the light
draws in charcoal
the sallow face
of my mother

She kindles the home fire
beneath the grate

a piece of kindling cracks
the scent of sap
the flame expands
and roars

in the window I see the sky
in the sky the sun
all around are your faces
their features
will never be reproduced

Notes Toward a Contemporary Love Poem

And yet white
is best described by gray
bird by stone
sunflowers
in December

the love poems of the past
favored the description of the body
this and that
eyelashes for instance

And yet red
should be described by gray

sun by rain
poppies in November
lips at night

the most palpable
description of bread
is the description of hunger
in it there is
a moist porous center
warm interior
sunflowers at night
breasts belly thighs of Cybele

a spring clear
transparent description
of water
is the description of thirst
of ashes
of desert
it induces mirage
clouds and trees step into
the mirror

Lack hunger
absence
of body
are the description of love
the contemporary love poem

Summer 1963

The Story of Old Women

I like old women
ugly women
mean women

they are the salt of the earth

they are not disgusted by
human waste

they know the flipside
of the coin
of love
of faith

dictators clown around
come and go
hands stained
with human blood

old women get up at dawn
buy meat fruit bread
clean cook
stand on the street
arms folded silent

old women
are immortal

Hamlet flails in a snare
Faust plays a base and comic role
Raskolnikov strikes with an axe

old women
are indestructible
they smile knowingly

god dies
old women get up as usual
at dawn they buy bread wine fish
civilization dies
old women get up at dawn
open the windows
cart away waste
man dies

old women
wash the corpse
bury the dead
plant flowers
on graves

I like old women
ugly women
mean women

they believe in eternal life
they are the salt of the earth
the bark of a tree
the timid eyes of animals

cowardice and bravery
greatness and smallness
they see in their proper proportions
commensurate with the demands
of everyday life
their sons discover America
perish at Thermopylae
die on the cross
conquer the cosmos

old women leave at dawn
for the city to buy milk bread meat
season the soup
open the windows

only fools laugh
at old women
ugly women
mean women

because these beautiful women
kind women
old women
are like an ovum
a mystery devoid of mystery
a sphere that rolls on

old women
are mummies
of sacred cats

they're either small
withered
dry springs
dried fruit
or fat
round buddhas

and when they die
a tear rolls down
a cheek
and joins
a smile on the face
of a young woman

1963

Dialogue

On the shores of the Black
Sea

I talked with a Russian poet
about poetry about Gogol
Shakespeare
Stalin fear
the wind blew our words away
right at the lips

the sun was setting
flooding with
blood
the water the sky the earth

Shakespeare the sea
carried on his back
ships loaded with grain

We talked about the crisis
of lyric poetry the novel the drama

Shakespeare inseminated Europe
buried the dead
waged wars

Smiled from ear to ear
asked in the voice of "poor Tom"
about the taste of dung
the salad of bay leaves
laughed at us kindheartedly

He held us in his palm
deposited us on the sand
and retreated into the sea
with open veins

1966

Non-Stop Show

Nowadays we make things without beginning or end
the conventional markers are no longer there they have been
forgotten
nowadays we create while falling leaving
We have no time we have no time to describe the wallpaper
the dress the eyes the lips the tree the house the sofa the leg
The clocks are ticking
someone is raising our children
there is still time
who is raising our children
we can still fight

to raise a new man
The clocks are ticking we smile politely
we have no time we have no time
for raising children
The possibilities for modern man
are limitless for raising children
It's still not too late
modern man flies through space
machines compose music
machines write poems
so there is poetry though there are no poets
there are young poets though there is no poetry
I thought

So then there are poets
So then there is poetry
so we eat roast though there is no meat
there are young poets
how unusual
surprising
there are young poets
there are young poets once again
it's quite startling
I suppose
that they themselves do not realize
what an unusual unexpected beautiful
startling funny monstrous
phenomenon they are
I thought
there would never again be
any young poets
and of course I was wrong
after all there are still stars tigers
nightingales cutlets women wardrobes tables cannons
novels abbots generals sonnets crawfish
politicians temples priests though there is no god
how good it is that there are young poets

In order to write in our time
one needs to hold back give in close off

turn deaf
in the past people wrote from excess
nowadays from lack
The possibilities for modern man are immense
dependent on constant anxiety
over whether it is not too late
for love for education for Esperanto for travel
for writing novels for children for beauty
for faith for life for death
We are immensely busy
We do not know our own children
I was retelling *Hamlet* to my son
The earth in July smells of honey
The earth unfolds
No need to make it dramatic we are solving a crossword puzzle
across a woman's name three letters long
down the name of an element
The earth smells of mushrooms
The frigidity of women
population growth
population growth in Shanghai
controlling flies mosquitoes sparrows
rats in Shanghai
Drawing rats out by playing the flute
and leading them into fire
or water was a common measure
practiced during the Middle Ages
The possibilities for modern man
are great or is it not too late
Birds are singing in the woods
Do . . . you . . . Dubonnet . . .
Taste enjoyment in every sip
Every sip will bring you calm . . . Every sip
refreshes and soothes
Finish the day . . .
bring on the night.
Yet isn't it too late
we can take advantage of every possibility
that girl's name is Eve
Eve's lips smell of tobacco in Paris

Das Spiel mit den Möglichkeiten
So one reads a newspaper a book
The frigidity of women is the fault of men
A Review of *Lolita*
"*Lolita*'s unprecedented success may be the most
sensational literary event of the past
decade. *Lolita*'s flavor does not lie in its descriptions
The love of a middle-aged man for a twelve-year-old
girl . . . Lolita is a symbol
of American civilization: young supple
vulgar immature . . ." A fragment of an article:
"A painting by a talented Spanish artist
was the spitting image of cow manure
lying in the road
flecked with black specks flies"
"at the same time another avant-garde movement
has emerged in English painting . . . the Marlborough
gallery held an exhibit of four members
of the group: Hoyland Plumb Turnbull and Stroud"

And yet in order to expand the range of possibilities
you leave your place of permanent residence
there beyond the woods is the sea
I just read I received an award
for poetic achievement
I ask my son whether he has read any of my poems
we head into the woods
nowadays we do everything simultaneously
we think about failures and defeats
we can still do something or is it not too late
we can escape
escape into the movies
we can hide in the movie theater
Never Let Go West Side Story Lolita
Vertigo I saw *Lolita* in Munich
Lolita this *Lolita* is a very long and boring
film starring a superb actor who is bad
in this film Lolita is an icicle
a girl devoid of underarm hair
like a doll He is a college professor or something

Lolita is a cruel naked doll lacking hair
both there and there
this dull axe this boring
melodrama has been showing for months in the largest
movie theater in Munich The Royal-Theater
Munich München
Italia Bar Harem-Bar Haremsfrauen
Bongo Bar Tai-Tung Beste Koche aus Chungking
La-Boheme Schaschlik Bockwurst Riesenwurst
Intermezzo Striptease à la Paris
Moulin Rouge Bomben Varieteprogramm
Die Zwiebel Lola Montez Bar Pique Dame
Nuremburg Bratwurstglöckl Restaurant
Weiß- und Bratwürste Hühner-Gustl
Schweinwürstl etc Playboys Bierhalle
Stachelschweine Schwabing
On parle français Eve Schöne Frauen
English spoken here cooks from Chungking
München Alte Pinakothek Alte Pinakothek
Alte Pinakothek
Cranach the Younger
Frans Hals Dürer
Mars and Venus Surprised by Vulcan
Boucher
Konditorei Bierhalle
at the Feldherrnhalle Bierhalle
at the Feldherrnhalle
Feldherrnhalle Feldherrnhalle
In Munich
a voice touched me from out of the darkness
words uttered
in my native tongue
uttered by a stranger
without a face
holding a beer mug
who was it a Ukrainian a Serb a Czech
a Pole a German an emigrant a Gestapo agent
who learned a few dozen Polish words
during the Occupation
an informer a soldier a torturer a victim

in the blink of an eye
I found myself on a dissecting table
bare bound immobilized
my corporeal covering was opened up again
they removed my innards
brain heart nest full of murder victims
in this streetside self-serve
lunchomat
I saw the face of an enemy mug of a dog
of a fascist a *Führer* a rat an enemy
his fingers tightening around
a throat a heart
his hand cold and dirty
the same words fell from his lips
But just then
in the hum of human voices and the warmth of the neon lights
in the eyes of women in the smiles
in the warm hum of life in shit
in the steaming entrails in the excrement
in the smell of beer and sausage in the dung
In the sounds of mechanical music
In the breasts and buttocks in heaven in miracle
Bratwurst Weißwurst Schweinwurst
Wienerwald Chungking
Crispy Chicken
authentic Munich sausage products
Pschorr Beer Dance Bar MADISON
I fell I crawled I bled
I crawled in the gutter I laughed
In the neon lights of the Non-stop-show
in the sounds of black music
in the darkness again
I covered my face
hatred filled me death mirth
the mirth of death dreaming laughter
the death of mirth the death of a dream

Nymphenburg Castle
park in the fog
statues and trees in the fog

the water's mirror surface fallen leaves silence baroque in the fog
in the autumn fog
the face of my German friend
Nymphenburg Castle
nymphen where the alleys lead
lost in the fog
out of the fog walks an old man
out of the fog walks a young woman
I look at the park the fog
at the castle the fog
I look into the eyes of my friend in the fog
there are woods
beyond the woods is a sea
there is a sea
we're solving a crossword puzzle
suddenly
it's clear the possibilities are limited
can one still become a saint
or is it too late
for posthumous exoneration
it's a long wait after all

I left for this secluded place
a week ago
throughout these days I've had the feeling
that there is no world beyond these woods
I now know that to leave our world
is not allowed
to distance oneself
is not allowed
in the past one could leave for the desert
now there's a need to be ever present
everybody is ever present
to leave our world is not allowed
not even for a day
everything must be interconnected

yesterday I tried to describe the sea
yesterday I did not yet
lack the courage

to describe the sea a dead man's face
a tree the earth the sun an apple
reality has the searing heat of the sun
dreams the gentleness and quiet of the moon
Nabokov's
Lolita
lolita
my body
is a forty-year-old domesticated
animal
spring opens up
gives dark signs
at dusk birds cry inside me
with round breasts
with round white breasts
with round blind breasts
with blind breasts
with white blind breasts
the love poems of the past favored the description of the body
the love poem proper the contemporary love poem
is to my mind not the description of a woman's
body but the description of the lack of a woman the best
the most nutritious the most palpable
description of bread is the description of hunger
in Khara-Khorum in the temple of the god of love
women as if put on a spit
with their mouths open
I'm forty-one
I sit at the table I look out the window
bright rain in the dark crowns
of trees
down below
golden lupines rain I summarize *Hamlet*
for my son
I tell him about the ghost who
about the rat behind the arras
about the gray-bearded prattler
I think of the
queen mother's thighs smooth as milk
about the desecrated nuptial bed

and so on and so forth
I won't say a word about
the question from Hamlet's soliloquy
it is too cruel a joke
for modern man

I hear a voice speaking to me
I hear myself speaking to me
You were mistaken
you should make peace
it's time
I'm forty-one already forty-two
truly you should make peace
should reestablish the torn threads the ties that bind
after all there is poetry again
everything will be again
How slowly I forget

I'm still speaking I keep on speaking
I remember that something should connect
with something else
express something
but I do not know to what end

gently smiling beaming face
the big warm womb patiently awaits the return of the prodigal
son my return

I set out from my home I left
my home my nest I left the womb
now I'm to return and press my face
close my eyes and lips seal my ears with wax
positive pleasant
pure poet

April–December 1963

My Poetry

justifies nothing
explains nothing
renounces nothing
encompasses no whole
fulfills no hope

creates no new rules of the game
takes no part in merriment
has a defined place
it must occupy

if it's not esoteric
if it's not original
if it doesn't awe
apparently it's as it should be

it obeys its own imperative
its own capabilities
and limitations
it loses against itself

it can neither take the place of
nor be replaced by any other
open to everyone
devoid of mystery

it has many goals
it will never achieve

1965

From

Regio,

1969

Homework Assignment on the Subject of Angels

Fallen
angels

look like
flakes of soot
abacuses
cabbage leaves
stuffed with black rice
hail
painted red
blue flames
with yellow tongues

fallen angels
look like
ants
moons wedged beneath
the green fingernails of the dead

angels in heaven
look like the inner thighs
of an underage girl

like stars
they shine in shameful places
they are pure like triangles and circles
with silence
inside them

fallen angels
are like the open windows of a morgue
like cows' eyes
like the skeletons of birds
like falling planes
like flies on the lungs of fallen soldiers
like streaks of autumn rain
connecting lips with birds taking flight

over a woman's palm
wander
a million angels

devoid of belly buttons
they type on sewing machines
long poems in the shape
of a white sail

their bodies can be grafted
onto the trunk of an olive tree

they sleep on ceilings
falling drop by drop

1964–1968

Autumnal

When it rains
I lie flat spread out distant
in a fog

I feel wet twigs
of blackthorn
stretched out under my skin
gnarled prickly
black

the capillarity
of blood vessels
of the stems of plants

up flows blood rust
bile patina
and colors the plain

on the rim
of the coal basin
a ploughman with a horse
forms a pastoral image
spread out forgotten

Grass

In the seams of walls
there
I grow
where they're placed
where they meet
where they arch

there I lodge
a blind seed
scattered by the wind

I spread patiently
in the cracks of silence
waiting for the walls to fall
and return to earth

then I will cover
faces and names

1962

July 11, 1968. Rain

A sieve of rain lengthens thickens
over house over field over forest

same view
as in 1967
only in the place
where lupines grew
rye fades in color

closely spaced raindrops
peck away at the tin windowsill
the same view
only without the white
shepherd dog
Bari was killed
and skinned
his doghouse was dismantled
its place overgrown by grass

and he was such a faithful dog
so obedient
he loved to eat and was so thankful
for every bite
every scrap

and he really knew how to be happy
how to greet you how to look you in the eye

* * *

Will something bad happen to me?

nothing bad will happen to me
I'll live through it all

how many times can a modern man
lose dignity

well then
shortly after this whole
history ends,
history with a small h
I'll get to work
what? yes
I'll get back to work
yes! I'll start learning Chinese
is it worthwhile
absolutely

the great patriot
poet Lu You
who lived from
1125 to 1210
when the Mongols were conquering
China
wrote
9300 poems
back then in China
people wrote poems
from top to bottom
from left to right
using no punctuation
not even a period

January 1968

From

Without a Title,

Poems from 1971–1976

* * *

ten years ago
I shouted at her

she went away
in shoes made of
shiny black paper

don't try to explain yourself
—she said—
you don't need to

in an empty
hospital corridor
I shouted at her

it was a hot July day
the oil paint
was peeling off the walls

the linden trees were fragrant
in a city park
covered in soot

I a godless man
wanted to cry forth a meadow for her
when dying and short of breath
she pushed away
at an empty and frightful netherworld

she returned to her place in the village
for a split second
in her final hour
I begged for her to have
a tree
a cloud a bird

I see her small feet
in oversized paper
funeral shoes

there I sat between
table and coffin
I a godless man yearned for a miracle
in this gasping industrial
city in the second half
of the twentieth century

drawn out of me
into the sunlight
all of this cries

* * *

the face of the motherland

motherland is the land of childhood
the place of birth
that is the small most near
motherland

city town village
street house backyard
first love
woods on the horizon
graves

in childhood one learns
flowers herbs grains
animals
fields meadows
fruits words

the motherland smiles

at first the motherland
is something close by
an arm's length away

it's only later that it grows
hurts
bleeds

From

A Traumatic Tale,

1979

* * *

I waded through the dream
with difficulty
until waking
in warm streams
of tears of words
Mother came toward me
Don't be afraid you are in the soil I said
nobody will harm you hurt you touch you
Mother in her fright
cuddled up to me
Mother don't be afraid you are in the soil
you are within me nobody will touch you
put you down or hurt you
I waded through the dream with difficulty
a Shadow stood before me

Photograph

today I received an old postcard
from a distant land
with a view of Erbalunga

I had never heard of this place
and I don't know where it is
nor do I want to know

Erbalunga

yesterday I received
a photograph of my mother
from 1944

in the photograph
she is still young beautiful
with a gentle smile

but on the back
I read the inscription
written in her hand:
"1944 was a cruel year for me"

in 1944
my older brother
was murdered by the Gestapo

we hid his death
from Mother

but she saw through us
and hid it
from us

The Boat

Don't cry
after all you didn't love him
he is an object
to be carried out of the house

windows discreetly ajar

in my black suit
in a boat
without oars
he leaves this world
Father
floats away

wooden casket
caught in flowers
green spruce wreaths
paper ribbons

Father lived
ninety years
he died in February 1977

don't cry

after all I did love him
beneath my eyelids a tiny image
Father carrying a green tree
treestand and axe
wading
through deep snow

colorful paper chains lie on the table
stars tinsel

may the soil grant him peace

From

On the Surface and Inside a Poem,

1983

I Am Noman

the dogs leap on Actaeon

On the 24th of May 1945
at three PM
he was moved
to a detention center

Ich bin Niemand
Mein Name ist Niemand
I am noman
my name is noman

I recognized him by his glasses
and his stubble
he was sixty years old at the time

wearing army fatigues
and soldier's boots

belts and laces
were taken away
from those put in the cage

on hot days
he paraded around in olive green
skivvies and tank top

the bars of the cage were reinforced

he said an anthology of lyric poetry
he found in the latrine
saved him from madness
that from the gates of death
that from the gates of death:
Whitman or Lovelace found
on the jo-house seat at that
in cheap edition!
Whitman liked oysters

I make a pact
with you Walt Whitman

I have detested you
long enough
I come to you
as a grown child
Who has had a pig-headed
father

I am noman
do you know a noman

a poet is a beast
immersed in the world
that's why he's so uncertain
about the world

and walked back and forth
inside the cage
without casting a glance
outside

then they let him
loose

he trampled
a circular path in the grass
which did not lead
to a watering hole

the dance of the intellect
among words

he found a handle
from an old broom
in his hands
the handle turned into
a sword
a tennis racket

a pool cue
a walking stick

a hearing
before the court
of the District of Columbia
February 13th 1946

Here sits Mr. Pound
Would you like to get up and present yourself
To the court
Thank you

—*Do any of you know Mr. Pound*
—*I do*
—*And did what poetry you did read of his make good sense?*
—*I think what I read was all right*
—Do you think that his delusions of grandeur and
high opinion of himself are
something particularly abnormal?
—Not in the case of a poet
—He is one of the greatest poets
—Yes
—*Does he understand that he is charged with treason in this court?*
—*He has a feeling that he has the key*
to the peace of the world
through the writings of Confucius which he translated
—*Do you think he suffers from delusions of any kind?*
—Yes. I think that he suffers from *both delusions of grandeur*
and delusions of persecution
both of which are characteristic of what we call
the paranoid condition

From death row
he was moved
to "*The Gorilla Cage*"

a poet is a beast
immersed in the world
that's why he's so uncertain
about the world

147

the dogs leap on Actaeon
he sat in a cage
for wild animals

during the day
huddled in a corner of the cage
at night
in the glare of the searchlights

the guards were silent

sometimes a passing soldier
stopped
looked at the strange specimen
poet beast traitor
"the father of modern literature"

would toss into the cage
cigarettes chocolate fruit
and then move on
the old man muttered
Usura usura usura
Rothschild Roosevelt Morgenthau
Usura usura usura
would praise Hitler's massacres
il miglior fabbro

Ich bin Niemand
Mein Name ist Niemand
I am noman
my name is noman

the dogs leap on Actaeon

love thy neighbor was practiced by
those who rejected the letter of the law

All I ever did was commit errors
words became void of meaning
awakened
I'm surprised

Elpenor, how art thou come to this dark coast?
Cam'st thou afoot, outstripping seamen?
And he in heavy speech:
"Ill fate and abundant wine. I slept in Circe's ingle . . .
A man of no fortune, and with a name to come."

SINGING FROM THE CAGE

Chi può	He who can
non vuo	does not want to
Chi vuo	He who wants to
non può	cannot
Chi sa	He who knows
non fa	does nothing
Chi fa	He who does
non sa	knows nothing
e cosi la vita se ne va!	and so life goes!

The Poet While Writing

The Poet while writing
has his back
to the world
to the disorder
of reality

The Poet while writing
is defenseless
easily startled
ridiculed frightened

he has emerged
left the animal
kingdom
one can see
on the drifting sands
prints of his birdlike feet

still ringing from afar
are voices words
the grainy laughter
of women

he must not
look
back

tossed onto the surface
empty he roams about
the apartment

he covers his face
astonishment
written all over it
a smile strays

still
he cannot answer
the simplest questions

he has heard
the breath of eternity
quickened
irregular

November 1979

They Came to See a Poet

they came to see a poet
and what did they see?

they saw a man
sitting in a chair
hiding his face

pausing a moment he said
too bad you didn't come
twenty years ago

then one of them
replied
but we hadn't been born
yet

I look at
four faces
reflected in the clouded mirror
of my life
from far away
I hear
their voices pure and strong

what are you working on at the moment
what are you up to, sir

I'm up to nothing
I reply
for fifty years I have been readying myself
for this difficult task
so that when "I'm up to nothing"
I mean NOTHING
—the sound of laughter—
when I am doing nothing
I'm in the middle of things
I clearly see those
who have chosen action

I see run-of-the-mill action
coming before run-of-the-mill thought

run-of-the-mill Gustav
turning into
run-of-the-mill Konrad

run-of-the-mill columnist
into run-of-the-mill moralist

I hear
run-of-the-mill conversation
between run-of-the-mill people

the run-of-the-mill envelops masses and elites

and this is only the beginning

Love Toward the Ashes

What sprouts out of the ashes of
Samuel Beckett?

somewhere in this space is
his fading breath
and then a motionless utterance

in the beginning was the word
in the end the body

What decomposes? What suffers?
meat still full of love
spoils in time
stinks
one has to bury it

Ms. Peggy
(in a "memoir devoid of tact")
spoke of how he never got out of bed
before noon
"Oblomov" she called him
I am dead he would say
but Peggy says
they had
a great love affair

More Pricks Than Kicks
this title got him driven out
of Ireland
when I think of him
and I think of him often
I sense that out of his body
out of his jacket out of his pants
seagrass grows
just like out of an old mattress
lying in a dumpster
in a blind alley
but he did make a move after all
took his bed
flew to Berlin
and directed
three
of his own plays

iron discipline
every move calculated
in time and space
every creak of the floor
every breath on the stage
and in the audience
every hair on the head

he did not grant interviews
for hours he talked about soup
with his maid

sometimes I hear his fading breath
(his laughter never
reaches me)
as if the fur coat of Sucky Molly
were yawning shedding fur

and instead of
Virginia Woolf's
famed "birds of Paradise"
the room is filled with flies

Narcissus looked
in the mirror
and saw the head
of a predatory bird
of course he had parents of some sort
alas! even James Joyce
had mother father wife children
as happens in this vale of tears

Some time ago I read his poems
"sans voix parmi les voix"
"among the voices voiceless"
poems like any other
but who doesn't write poetry

too bad we will never
meet because I admired him

for the fact that he
breathed so calmly
awaiting the end of the world

but even he begins to bore

1982

On Felling a Tree

        In memory of Jarosław Iwaszkiewicz, author of Gardens

In the sphere of crowns
there is constant anxiety

a tree marked
for felling
with a white sign of annihilation
was still breathing
the boughs and branches
clung
to clouds floating away

the leaves were trembling wilting
sensing death

Trees do not move
from place to place
looking for food
they cannot escape
the saw the axe

in the sphere of crowns there is
constant anxiety

the felling of a tree is an execution
devoid of ceremony

a chainsaw
puffing sawdust
enters as fast as lightning
the bark the pulp the heart

struck in the side
the tree fell
its dead weight crushing
grasses wild herbs
slender bright shoots
quivering spiderwebs

along with the tree
its shadow was lost
transparent
multivalent
an image
a sign
appearing
in the light
of the sun of the moon

hardworking roots
did not yet sense
the loss of the trunk
and crown

slowly
the death of the tree aboveground
reaches the world underground

the roots of neighboring trees
touch one another
form close contacts
fuse

Trees
the only living feeling beings
besides humans and animals

created in the image
and likeness of gods
cannot hide from us

Children born
painlessly in clinics
growing up
in discos
rent by artificial light
and sound
gazing into the TV screen
do not talk to
trees

Felled burnt
lying in a row
poisoned dead
the trees of childhood
in May
greening over our heads
in November
shedding leaves on graves
they grow within us
until death

July 1981

The Poet's Return

I fell asleep
a young man

it was snowing at night

I woke up an old
poet

between us
stretched a green meadow
covered in ash

I dreamt that I wrote poems

gnomes roses and linguists
appeared again
in the manicured gardens of poetry

Mejoró su nariz
y su vida!
I chuckled
She did improve her nose
and her life!

I dreamt that
I read my poems
in Mexico
that Jan Zych
hummingbird overhead
was speaking in Spanish

I saw
golden Tepotzotlán
eyeing itself in the mirrors
of day and night
drop after drop falling
into the ocean into the sky

I flew over the Atlantic
Face a volume of poetry
in my suitcase
along with shaving cream razor blades
salami toilet paper
cotton balls olive oil coffee envelopes
socks sweater cigarettes
silver ring
the Rain god a bar of soap
matches from the El Presidente Hotel

address book you have wings
jump

On awakening
what I read is anonymous
I have forgotten
what poetry is
other poets have been writing
my poems

A Poem

I wanted to describe
the falling of leaves
in Park Południowy

five white swans
standing on the water's foggy
mirror

I wanted to paint
black chrysanthemums
oxidized by frost

light on the lips
of a girl
passing by

I thought of poets
of the land of the middle
they had acquired the knowledge
of how to write perfect poems
they have faded away
but the light of their poems
reaches me
thousands of years later

a leaf touched the ground

I understood
weeping icons
the silence of music
the mystery of wounded poetry

upon returning home
my hand began to write
a poem
deaf and mute
wanted to come into being
to see the light of day
but I don't want to write it
I can hear it as it slowly
ceases to breathe

November 1982

All of a Sudden

All of a sudden I saw in a newspaper
something resembling a poem

letters words
that reminded me
of some other words
resembling those words

some metaphors
paper entrails
images collected
from the dumpster of history
from the dumpsters of poetry

stains words
swarmed
on newsprint
running

from each other

there was the name
of the author
the same name
that's him I thought
or is it not him

I started
rereading
from the beginning
but I did not understand

I did not understand anything
as if I had wandered
far from this place
from this language
from myself

November 1982

Chiaroscuro

When shadow falls
on my poem
I see light in it
faint stubborn
a life

tiny death
takes its first steps
matures quickly
grows
at night lies
on my heart
on my lips
like a sea chiseled
in black stone

you were screaming at night
dreadfully
frightfully
my wife says

it was death drilling corridors
within me a living being
death screaming within me
like a deserted cave
full of bones

When light falls
on my poem
I see death in it
a black grain
of ergot
in a golden head of wheat
which drifts off
beyond the horizon

September 1983

From

Bas-Relief,

1991

without

the greatest events
in a human life
are the birth and death
of God

father our Father
why
at night
like a bad father

without a sign without a trace
without a word

why have You forsaken me
why have I forsaken
You

life without god is possible
life without god is impossible

after all as a child
You were my sustenance
I ate the flesh
I drank the blood

maybe You forsook me
when I tried to spread
my arms
to embrace life
reckless
I spread my arms
and dropped You

or maybe You fled
unable to take
my laughter

You do not laugh

or maybe You have punished me
dim little man for my obstinacy
for pride
for
I tried to create
a new man
a new language

You have forsaken me without the sound
of wings of lightning
like a field mouse
like water absorbed by sand
busy distracted
I did not notice your escape
your absence
from my life

life without god is possible
life without god is impossible

March 1988–March 1989

* * *

poetry doesn't always
take the form
of a poem

after fifty years
of writing
poetry
may appear
to the poet
in the shape of a tree
a bird
flying away
light

166

it takes the shape
of lips
it nests in their silence

or it lives in a poem
devoid of form and content

October 13, 1988

* * *

In memory of Konstanty Puzyna

Time hastens
my time is up

what should I take with me
to the other shore
nothing

so is that
it
Mother

yes son
that's it

so that's all

that's all

so this is a life

yes all of it

1989

* * *

black stains are white

before the third
radiant
star
war

human imagination was taken away
along with the survival instinct
death nestled
in lettuce chives
green
the color of hope

a child was born
with two heads
a calf was born
with three legs

white stains are black
black stains are red

behind closed doors
beneath which sniff
a pack of journalists
smiling diplomats
roll dice
and read the future of the world
and the human race
from the entrails of fallen soldiers

a child was born
with four legs
a calf was born
with two wings

behind closed doors
politicians and generals
speak face-to-face
with a second face
painted over the first
faceless
they fight to save face

white stains are black
black stains are yellow

"Der Tod ist ein Meister aus Deutschland"

In memory of Paul Celan

"What good are poets in time of need?"

The gods deserted the world
leaving the poets behind
but the well-spring
drank our mouths dry
took away our speech

we travel and live
on the road
here and there

Antschel the wandering Jew
journeyed long
from Bukovina to Paris
gathering herbs along the way
and with the words Heidekraut
Erica Arnica
he would put words to sleep
set them in darkness

in der Hütte
Celan met
Martin Heidegger

entered
a woodland meadow
stood there beneath the stars
emerged from the night
"Der Tod ist ein Meister
aus Deutschland"
stood in the clearing
with a handful of grasses and flowers

but beneath the stone bridges
the waters of the Seine flowed on
with ineffable smile waited
a beautiful Stranger

Death mask

and he ripened
fell into the open womb
of the river
of death of forgetting

in a world
the gods had left
he was touched by living poetry
and he followed them

what question
did the poet ask the philosopher
what philosopher's
stone
lies by the path
to a hut in the woods

"Der Tod
ist ein Meister
aus Deutschland"

In the time that has come
after the time of need

after the departure of the gods
the poets are departing

I know that I shall wholly die
and from this flows
the small comfort

which gives me strength
to exist outside of poetry

1990

Conversation with a Friend

For a few months now
my Friend
Kornel Filipowicz
has been in the otherworld
while I continue on in this one

I do not believe in the afterlife
so I am trying to understand
your crossing the threshold
into the otherworld

I'm reading your book
trying to recall
just how our conversation
had ended

your silence your leaving
explained by death

I've tried
to defend
an independent poet writer
independent
of Warsaw London
Rome Moscow Paris
Kraków and Pacanów

we sit in silence for a while
an art we have learned
over our
44 years of friendship

the doorbell rings
Wisława enters
with smoked herring
(two smoked herring . . .
one for Mizia the cat
the other for Kornel)
the black cat sits
on the desk and looks into my eyes

I'm thinking that poems
from the otherworld
say nothing
about homeland
mother father brothers
are silent about Auschwitz
are silent about Katyń

are like trees
petrified

in my eyes
they grow over with green leaves
rustle
in this vale of tears
I still write
poems
leaving in them my tongue
together with my entrails

I say good-bye move away
slowly you close the door

I am on the staircase
I look back

"you can start writing me at Lea Street"
you say to me

Pig Roast

For Jerzy Nowosielski
a memento of our conversations about the killing of animals

"Remember that if the devil
wants to kick somebody, he won't do it
with his horse's hoof,
but with his human foot."

in a Swiss daily
I read an article
titled "Arme Schweine"
Poor pigs

how these innocent creatures
must suffer anticipating death
yet aren't our Polish pigs
as sensitive
as their Swiss sisters

En route to the slaughterhouse
they often die of heart attacks

in our country the pig roast is linked
with birth and death
with christenings funerals
and even first communion

In *Politics* I read an article
about transplanting a pig's heart
into a young man

"Of all things why did you settle
on a pig's heart?" asks the journalist.
"Based on size considerations,"
replies Professor Zbigniew Religa
from the Silesian School of Medicine;
"these were young individuals
weighing from 180 to 220 pounds
such that their hearts would be of human size . . .
and the Church condones
all transplants except for
brains
and reproductive organs . . . "

long live the pig!
friend of man
I sound this cheer
from the depths of my (human) heart

long live all pigs
eaten by humanity
since the dawn of creation!

how many pigs' hearts kidneys
how many pigs' feet
will be transplanted
by the end of the century

I ask as a moralist

can we find even one
man who would give his heart brain
or kidney to an ailing pig

when will humanity mature
into such love
that we could say
my sister sow

when will we build in Geneva or New York
in front of the headquarters of the United Nations
a monument
to a pig with her young

the competition for such a monument
I hereby declare open

From

always a fragment,

1996

Francis Bacon or
Diego Velázquez in the dentist's chair

for thirty years
I have been hot on Bacon's heels

I've looked for him in pubs galleries
butcher shops
in newspapers art books photographs

once I met him in the Kunsthistorisches Museum in Vienna
he was standing in front of a portrait
of infanta Margarita
Infantin Margarita Teresa in blauem Kleid
Diego Rodríguez de Silva y Velázquez

I got him I thought
but it was someone else

after death
after Francis Bacon's departure
I put him under glass
I wanted to look at the painter
from every angle

given
his natural tendency
to escape to disappear
to drink
to migrate
through time and space
from pub to pub
a baroque *putto*
who lost a hat
and a red sock
I had to
immobilize him

for a few weeks
I went to the Tate Gallery
locked myself in with him
and devoured him with my eyes

digested his terrifying
masterpiece of meat copulation of carcasses
withdrawn into myself
I continued my dialogue
with Saturn who was busy
eating his own children
Man is killed just like an animal
I've seen truckloads of chopped-up people
who will never be saved
I wrote in 1945

under the influence of booze Bacon
became warm sociable
generous hospitable
treated his friends to
champagne caviar
turned into an angel
wing dipped
in a beer mug

most of my paintings he'd say—
are the work of a man
in a state of Anxiety

while painting a triptych
I turned to drink for help
it only helped once
he mumbled
while fingerpainting on the glass
Lager Beer Lager Beer
in 1962 I was painting
the crucifixion
sometimes hung over
barely aware of what I was doing
but that time it helped

Bacon achieved the transformation
of a crucified figure
into dead meat hanging
he rose from the table and said softly
yes sure we're meat
we're potentially dead meat
whenever I walk into a butcher shop
I always think
how amazing it is that it's not me hanging from the hook
it must be pure chance
Rembrandt Velázquez
well yes they believed in the resurrection
of the body they'd pray before painting
but we're all acting
modern art has become a game
ever since Picasso we've all been acting
some better some worse

have you seen Dürer's drawing
hands folded in prayer
sure they drank ate and murdered
raped and tortured
but they believed in the resurrection of the body
and life everlasting

too bad . . . we . . .
he didn't finish and left for parts
known only to himself
years passed
in hunting down Bacon
I was helped by Adam
poet translator
the owner of Shorthand
who lives in London
and Norwich
on the twelfth of June 1985
he wrote me:
Dear Tadeusz,
Today I saw a huge Bacon exhibit
and I thought you would have

enjoyed it immensely. As for me I went reluctantly.
I don't regret it though—the early gnawed-on heads
are effective in their color and composition.
But I wasn't taken with
the more recent paintings. As I wrote earlier
I'll be coming to Wrocław (. . .)
on the flip side is a reproduction of *Head IV*

but Adam I
can't tell
Bacon
He doesn't know Polish
and I don't know English

so tell him my first book was *Anxiety*
in 1947 I wrote:

rosy ideals
hang quartered
in butcher's booths (. . .)

in 1956 I wrote:

meat still breathing
filled with blood
nourishes
these perfect forms

they press so tightly around their prey
that even the silence does not seep
out (. . .)

both of us journeyed
through *The Waste Land*

Bacon said he likes
looking at his paintings through glass

he even likes Rembrandt
behind glass

he's not bothered by random strangers
reflected in the glass
blurring the picture
passing by
I
cannot stand paintings behind glass
I see myself there I remember one time
I saw a few Japanese
superimposed on Mona Lisa's smile
they were very agile
Gioconda was immobilized
in a glass coffin
after that adventure
I never went to the Louvre again
Gioconda smiled Gioconda's smile
Bacon locked up
Pope Innocent VI in a cage
then Innocent X
and Pius XII
Infanta Margarita in blue
a judge and a prosecutor
they all started screaming

in 1994
on February the fourteenth
Saint Valentine's Day
Francis Bacon appeared to me
on the glass of the TV screen
round head oval face
wrinkled suit
I listen to Bacon
I watch the portrait
the red face of Pope Innocent VI
the gentle features of the Infanta

I tried to show
the landscape of the oral cavity
but I failed
Bacon said
in the oral cavity I find

all the beautiful colors
of the paintings of Diego Velázquez

glass suppresses screams
I thought
Bacon conducted his surgical procedures
without an anesthetic
resembling the practice
of 18th-century dentists
Zahnextraktion
they also lanced abscesses boils and carbuncles
this won't hurt he'd say to the little Infanta
open your mouth please
unfortunately I don't have any anesthetics
this is going to hurt
little Infanta in the gynecologist's chair
Pope Innocent VI in the electric chair
Pope Pius XII in the waiting room
Diego Velázquez
in the dentist's chair
a friend *George Dyer*
before a Mirror—1968
or on the toilet seat . . .

I painted open mouths
Poussin's scream in Chantilly
and Einstein's scream on the stairs
I painted
on a canvas made of newspaper
on reproductions
in the corner of my studio
there was a pile of newspapers photographs
as a young man
in Paris I bought
a book on diseases of the oral cavity
Bacon talked to David Sylvester
and didn't pay any attention to me

I wanted to provoke him
so I asked if he had heard

of Sigmund Freud's rotting mouth
at the end of his life even his faithful
dog ran away
it couldn't stand the stench
why didn't you paint
a palate eaten
by a beautiful cancer
Bacon pretended he didn't hear

your models shriek
like clouds skinned alive
again you put pope
Innocent the something
in the oven
again you want
to administer
"die Applizierung" des Klistiers
to this dreamy well-mannered and painted
Infanta

I wanted to ask Adam
for help but
Adam smiled
ate his tuna fish sandwich
and drank a Heineken

tell him Adam
tell him
in English please
that to me a closed mouth
makes the most beautiful landscape

the lips of the Stranger from Florence
Andrea Della Robbia
Ritratto d'Ignota
Portrait of an unknown Woman

also tell him
that Franz Kafka was afraid of open
mouths and of teeth full of meat and gold crowns

I used this in my play *The Trap*
performed in Norwich
too bad Bacon didn't paint
a portrait of Eliot suffering
from inflammation of the periosteum
his face wrapped in a checkered
handkerchief

Adam was now eating
a smoked salmon sandwich
Tadeusz—you're already on your third one
I warned you
Guinness is strong
ask Francis
if he knows what Wondratschek said
about the mouth and teeth
Adam put away his Shorthand

*"The mouth is suddenly
tired of the teeth"*
Wondratschek said

Bacon told a beer mug:
I never managed
to paint a smile
I had always hoped
that I would be able to paint mouths
the way Monet painted
a sunset

but I painted
mouths filled with screams and teeth

crucifixion? again I repeat
it's the only painting
I painted drunk
neither drinking nor drugs
helps painting
one simply gets talkative
or just plain chatty

good-bye Francis Bacon
I wrote a long poem about you
I won't be looking for you
the end period
ah! but still the title of this poem
Francis Bacon
or
Diego Velázquez
in the dentist's chair
not bad
none of the Irish
or English critics
or poets
came up with
a title like that
perhaps needlessly
I added to it
such a long poem
but drinking beer
one simply gets talkative
or just plain chatty

February 1994–March 1995

* * *

---

an empty room

empty?
but I am in it

I am I write
I listen to the silence

on the pillow the hollow
left by your head
being filled
being smoothed
by time

what would I miss

Wiesława's smile
when she says good morning
or good night

or when she says nothing

when she closes the door behind me
or opens it
after a long journey
or upon my return
from a land far off to her
where I was constructing a poem

what would I miss

the quiet between our faces
and words left
unspoken
because what is sacred
between human beings
constantly seeks
expression

what would I miss

"my whole life"
and something else
grand wonderful
beyond words
beyond body

From

always a fragment. recycling,

1998

poet emeritus

for Czesław Miłosz

he sits down on a bench
takes off his glasses
closes his eyes

wipes off his glasses
opens the newspaper takes a look at the world
folds the paper gets up

loses his balance
leans on his cane
reads the writing
on the bench

walks talks to himself

speaks with the dead
poets

two women
come up to him
they ask whether he reads the Bible
believes in hell
the end of the world paradise on earth

he smiles nods his head
in his old age he prefers
speaking with people
who are silent

he walks away
sits on a bench
looks at the clouds

then a raven
flies up to him
strokes a black feather
across his lips
seals them
and flies away

1996

From Mouth to Mouth

Idea

its language
as beautiful and twisted
as the serpent
in Eden

from the philosopher's mouth
it comes out clean
as far
from "reality"
as soul from body

then politicians preachers
activists
take it on their tongues

chewing it up
and spitting it out onto the heads
of the people

the journalist
takes the idea
from out of the politician's mouth
seasons it with saliva
arrogance
provocation
and excretes it through
"the mass media"

the idea grows in the mouth
reaches the street

takes to the streets
staggers
like a drunken prostitute
from right to left

the idea passes
from hand to hand
in the eyes
of a dumbfounded world
turns into a murder weapon

and what does the philosopher do

he says nothing and leaves
never looking
back

as if he did not hear the words:

Not that which goes into the mouth
defiles a man;
but that which comes out of the mouth
defiles a man. . . .

In a Hotel

under the ceiling
I hear a nightingale

a human
sways on a string
black

so that's how things were
for Yesenin
in the fall
winter spring

everything as distant
as a nebula

as the old-fashioned
love for a woman

whose lips
alighted on the poet's hand

fleeting
like the wings of a butterfly

nothing lasts forever
every moment passes
the beautiful
and the terrifying

recycling

Was ist Recycling? Die Wiederverwendung
bereits einmal oder mehrfach benutzter
Rohstoffe zur Gewinnung neuer Produkte

What is recycling? The reuse
of raw materials, used
once or multiple times, to make
new products

I

FASHION (1944–1994)

his outfit consisted of
a watchman's cap
a nightgown lacking buttons
a small woman's sweater
pants spattered with red paint
old shoes
one of them worn through
the other a lady's slipper
that didn't even fit

fifty years later

for casual wear
natural fibers are back in vogue
wool blends are in
with polyester and nylon
woven to resemble
Grandma's hand-knit
vests sweaters hats and scarves
dark colors are most popular
black gray silver steel
dirty shades of orange
sky blues and yellows are eclipsing
the loud colors which up till now
have reigned on the ski slopes

she sports torn long johns
to match a man's shirt
torn old pants
and a Russian soldier's jacket

wears a star on white canvas
gentile women wear a red triangle
rags on their shaved heads
I feel like I'm at
a costume ball
the orchestra plays *Highlander, aren't you sad*

some of the women defecated into
their soup bowls

fifty years later

even the most stylish women
have trench coats or sailor's peacoats
glittering with two rows of buttons
hanging in their wardrobes
a sailor's jumper a boatswain's jacket
a bomber jacket an officer's cap
pilot's jumpsuits always find
faithful fans it's not just
teenage punks
who go for the military look

he looked inside the mouth under the tongue
between fingers and toes
into the rectum
inside the ears

*"Guess who's wearing
the pants this summer?"*

*The designers have come up
with a number of different styles:*

*Cigarette-pants, the Marlene-Dietrich-look
Hippie-chic, Gucci-dresses
bright yellow hip-huggers
with a floral pattern
go great with bare midriff tops
and pullovers*

This is how they addressed women in Auschwitz
du vollgestopfter Strumpf—you stuffed stocking
du alte Hexe alte Kanone—you old witch, old cannonball
alter Hut alter Fetzen alte Krippe—old hat, old rags, mangy manger
alte Gazette—old newspaper
du Scheißladen Scheißkübel—you shit shop shit crock
alte Waschkommode alte Ziege—old washstand old nanny goat
alte Zitrone—old lemon
Krematoriumsfigur—Crematorium fodder

are you a man
who would like to rendezvous on
planet woman?

strong, sensual, sexy
attractive academic blonde
are you into theater
music literature dancing skiing
tennis sauna travel hiking

a Woman meets a man
a Woman meets a woman
a Man meets a woman
a Man meets a man

come on
join the fun

a tasteful fuzz has appeared
on her head recently shaven
for a film shoot
and her beautiful body, framed
by a pink bikini,
is wrapped in a large towel

the biggest mistake
is mixing warm shades with cool ones
e.g., warm orange lipstick
with cool pink nail polish
warm poppy-red

with cool cherry
copper lipstick
with primrose nail polish

II

GOLD

Aurea prima sata est aetas (. . .)

the first age was the golden age
ages passed
along came the twentieth century

the twentieth century is passing
the Christian world
is nearing its end
strange signs
have appeared in the heavens and on earth

strange signs have appeared
on gold ingots
in the safes of the Riksbank
the central bank of Sweden
gold started to weep
bloody tears
to hide this
the Riksbank asked
the Swiss central bank
to remove all German
markings
from the gold ingots
and replace them
with the seal of Sweden

gold started to talk
in the Federal Reserve Bank
in the Bank of England in London
in New York
Paris in Banque de France
in Madrid

in Lisbon
a golden silence had descended
upon the capitals of Europe and the Americas
then it began to melt
the gold bricks gold ingots
gold bars
gold coins
gold laundered in Europe and America
started to talk
erupt in stains
bleed
vaults
are as tightly sealed as gas chambers
but the grinding of teeth can be heard
muffled cries
the stifling stench of road kill
seeps out of the safes
pus from corpses oozes out
and blood
gold laundered in Switzerland
decomposes and rots
in aseptic Sweden

it contains gold teeth
gold crowns gold rings
with diamond eyes
eyeglass frames hair
fountain pens gasps
the banks reveal
the secrets of their bosom
banks the temples of the golden calf
monumental goldscheissers
excrete
impurities

gold sand
flows through the hourglass

Press Secretary
for the Holy See
Joaquin Navarro-Valls

could not confirm
information
provided by the American
television network A&E
that the Vatican had "set aside"
200 million Swiss francs
mainly in gold coins
looted by Croatian
fascists in
World War II
Croatian fascists who
mass-murdered
Serbs Jews and Gypsies
smuggled around three hundred and fifty million
Swiss francs out of Yugoslavia
toward the end of the war
the British managed to seize
around one hundred and fifty million Swiss francs
but the rest
found its way to the Vatican
from there
rumor has it
it was transferred to Spain and Argentina

long poems
Newsweek: *Nazi-Gold*
Also In Portugal
das lange Gedicht
the long poem
Israel has joined the dispute
over the money
of Holocaust victims
it's not the first time
Jewish organizations have threatened action against
Swiss banks
but maybe
the Holocaust never happened

increasingly one reads
in German neo-Nazi newspapers
in American papers
in reprints
of foreign sources in Polish-language nationalist papers
that the Holocaust never happened

increasingly one sees on the walls of our cities
graffiti in Polish
"gas the Jews" and in German *"Juden raus"*
these are insensitive teenagers
badly raised boys kids
who draw the Star of David
hanging from a noose

das lange Gedicht
during the Nazi occupation
my friend Kazimierz Wyka
wrote for the sake of posterity
"The means by which Germans liquidated Jews
rests on their conscience.
Reaction to those means,
however, rests on our conscience.
A gold tooth extracted from a corpse
will bleed forever,
even when no one remembers
where it came from (. . .)"

the gold ingots soften
a poem gets longer decomposes
"Worst suspicion
immediately after World War II,
Switzerland might have
minted coins
out of gold dental fillings
taken from Holocaust victims,
possibly aware of their source (. . .),
according to the BBC"
but the Holocaust never happened

my friend
Kazimierz Wyka
must have heard this "funny" saying
in Nazi-occupied Poland
"With Hitler came a perk: he taught the Jews to work"
Kazimierz Wyka one of the righteous
wrote a book *The Excluded Economy: Life As If*
I don't know whether this book
is required reading
in Polish schools
I don't know how long we will have to wait
for the ladies and gentlemen from the National Ministry
of Education
to put this title on the list
of required readings
(they may not have read this book
or even heard of it)
Kazimierz Wyka never planted a tree in the Holy Land
gold bars and gold ingots
bare their teeth
the skulls keep silent the sockets speak

executive director of the World Jewish Congress Elan Steinberg
insists that among the ingots
of monetary gold are
some melted out of jewelry coins
and even the gold teeth of Holocaust victims
but no concrete evidence
has yet been brought forth
or perhaps an error was made
an heir to the Bertrams
orchard owners near Wyszków held
that his grandfather had sizable deposits
in Swiss banks
but perhaps the Holocaust never happened
shortly after the war
gold diggers appeared
armed with spades and pickaxes
pans and sieves
they were searching for gold veins

gold sand
gold teeth
in gold-bearing Auschwitzes
Majdaneks Treblinkas
they searched through the ashes
through the entrails of our
common mother earth
searching for gold gold gold

but the Holocaust never happened

it was made up by Jewish
usurers bankers and Communists
in cahoots with the Gypsies
Madonnas are weeping bloody tears
only the Gypsy Madonna doesn't weep
the silence of the world is golden
in the Holy Land the righteous plant trees
the sacred grove the young wood
is turning green
trees grow toward the light
the great sacred wood begins to move
it advances toward
the youth of the world
the nations carefully count
their dead their murdered
gassed maimed
buried alive hung
add subtract
multiply divide weigh
but the Holocaust never happened

no one remembers anymore
the weight of a human tear
the price of tears is falling on the stock market
there is a panic in the market
gold goes up gold falls
who talks about the tear of a child
oh yeah Dostoyevsky

Heidegger
writing about contemporary mechanized
agricultural production
mentioned in passing
the production of corpses
in concentration camps
and gas chambers

the counting of
Jews Gypsies Germans
Ukrainians Poles Russians continues
sometimes the numbers do not add up
ashes mingled with earth
rise up against one another
on account of the living
they separate and fight

porcelain Madonnas weep
bloody tears
Jewish Muslim Algerian
headless mothers
march ahead shouting
Raphael's Gypsy Madonna
does not weep does not speak to me
beautiful full of grace

the living forest of the righteous
advances
toward the temples of the golden calf
toward the banks and turns to stone

out of the strongboxes the safes
the armored vaults
a pus oozes
gold pure as tears
turns into roadkill
bares its teeth
and the count resumes

long poems
in the safes of the Riksbank of Sweden
there are still
around seven tons of gold looted
by Nazi Germany
which the Third Reich used
to pay Sweden for iron ore
ball bearings
and other strategic supplies
but the Holocaust never happened
representatives of the Riksbank declare
that they long ago got rid of all
the "dirty" gold in Sweden
in 1946 seven tons of gold
were returned to Belgium
and in 1954 six tons
were returned to Holland
during World War II Sweden
was neutral
and it seems that the Holocaust never happened
the world's silence was golden

das lange Gedicht

P.S.

what a long poem! it drags on
and on doesn't its author get bored
can't it all fit into
a Japanese haiku? No it can't.

III

MEAT

> *to Witold Zatoński*
> *in friendship*

Mad beef
mad cow disease
bone-in Madness

the new scandal over beef
Danger on Your Plate
Steering Clear of Steak and Roast
Mad Cows in Hong Kong
Swine Plague in Tulip Country

BSE
Bovine Spongiform Encephalopathy
after a two-hour meeting
in Downing Street
Prime Minister J. Major in attendance
London suspends its slaughter program
the British minister of something or other
recommends—right before the elections—
roast beef hamburgers and steak
all over the TV and newspapers
pictures of the minister
consuming English beef
shown with his entire family
everyone's smiling and looking healthy

all happy families are alike
Leo Tolstoy once remarked
and quit eating meat

Paris expressed regret
over London's unilateral decision

the Blair government plans
to ban the sale of beef on the bone
ribs and chops
are soon to be taken off the market
"does this mean we shouldn't
eat any beef?" despairing
consumers ask

in Wales violent protests
over the glut of cheap
Irish beef
considered safe

Welsh farmers attack Irish trucks
and dump several tons of beef
into the sea

the report suggests that
PRIONS
carriers of mad cow disease
present in the nervous system
lead to
Creutzfeldt-Jakob disease in humans
they are also present in the nerve fiber
surrounding cow bones

Paris expressed regret

but in seven years
the BSE and CJD epidemics
will reach their height in Great Britain
most vulnerable are those who ate beef
in the late eighties
who stuffed themselves with
hamburgers
produced partly from the brain
spinal cord and other parts
of the cow's nervous system

between 1986
—when the disease was discovered—
and 1989 the British public consumed
the meat of approximately 446 thousand
infected animals
the British minister laughs
the German minister cannot decide
to eat or not to eat beef
the Danish minister of agriculture
Henrik Dam Kristensen
notes that the European Union
made a clear pact concerning
the slaughter program
minister Kristensen warns

London against exploiting
the issue of mad cow disease
in the upcoming election

the head of Germany's diplomatic service Klaus Kinkel
considered the decision "un-accept-able"
"this is a grave matter"
said the Russian Deputy Prime Minister and
Minister of Agriculture Viktor Khlystun
the Russian government announced
that 730 tons of British beef
banned from export under the pact
were nonetheless exported to Russia
via Belgium

the European Commission published
the report of an inspection
revealing that
1600 tons of British beef were illegally exported
to Spain France and Holland

Paris expressed regret
over London's unilateral decision

"The farmers' union president
calls on the public to support
an 'Extra Meatball Day
for healthy nutrition
from Schleswig-Holstein'"
the cows are laughing like mad

Kitty Kitty
a company that makes canned pet food
assures its clients it has never used
animal discards from Great Britain
in its products
but still the germ is transmitted
from beef to other living beings
on one farm minks went mad
in England a puma died
several antelope and forty-eight cats

the tabloids say
a princess went mad one day
and a cow in a barn
started to sing:
"in a meadow of grass and clover
in the county of Hannover
a handsome steer went insane
a sponge full of holes for a brain

the princess turned into a kook
and later turned out a book
the cow wagged its tail while dying
then expired along with its prions"

London accepts none of the blame
Prince Charles wondered aloud
at a meeting of ecologists whether someday BSE
might not be taken
for the revenge of nature
for violating its laws
he called for organic farming

European Union authorities ruled out
lifting the worldwide ban on
Britain's export of beef and livestock

France adopted a wait-and-see policy
Robert Will of Edinburgh
an expert on Creutzfeldt-Jakob disease
saw no evidence among the British population
of a categorical increase
in cases of damaged or porous
brains
but in Hong Kong
7 people died yesterday
who may have been afflicted
with Creutzfeldt-Jakob disease

due to sanctions from the Common Market
Switzerland had to liquidate
240 thousand cattle
and process them into feed
(and what happened to that feed?!)
contaminated cattle feed
made out of bonemeal
and the meat of dead livestock
caused an epidemic
while tending sheep a dog went mad too
a German shepherd in Scotland
bonemeal from cows
infected with the deadly BSE
was taken off the market

"just between us humans"
pigs and cows awaiting slaughter
should not see how
others are killed before them
because when a cow gets frightened
it secretes glycogen from its muscles and liver
and its meat turns tough and dark
even worse it can taste like soap
the same goes for pigs
pork from a frightened pig
is white watery tasteless

the European Commission stands by its plan
to liquidate 147 thousand "units"
older than thirty months
as was agreed upon in Florence
at a European Union summit

Paris expressed anxiety
meanwhile the deputy commissioner
Franz Fischler remarked in Strasbourg:

the possibility of BSE contamination cannot
be excluded in beef bouillon
and even sausages can

be contaminated with BSE
especially if cows' brains
have been used

Paris expressed regret

however good news
for alcoholics came from London
Dr. Hugh Rushton
prominent British expert
in the fight against balding reported
that one of the most effective ways
to preserve a thick head of hair
is the consumption of a large amount of alcohol
it was reported that bald men are very good lovers
integration demands quarantine
for cows sheep pigs dogs and cats
squirrels rhinoceroses ministers
commissioners CEOs
tulips chimpanzees parrots
Beware of imports!
Mommy mommy what about our Jell-O
it's not our Jell-O
it's an import
slaughtered infected lambs
were not tossed into the hellfire
but were turned into a new product
excellent bonemeal for beef cattle

There is no indication
that consumption in Poland will increase
in 2000 the average Pole will eat
8 kg of beef—wise Pole!
while a resident of the member states
will eat on average 20.5 kg of beef a year
the healthy Polish cow sings:
let there be war the world around
so long as there's peace within this town
so long as there's joy within this town
may peace and joy go round and round

France expressed mild
surprise

Felix Austria
the meaning of beef
(for Austrian cooking)
is almost strategic *(sic)*
Felix Austria there beef
is not only healthy
(raised locally of course)
but around the rump
a prion is not to be found
Beef—selling like hotcakes

evidently the pathogens
which lead to brain degeneration
are PRIONS
degenerated proteins
which, in their healthy form
are found in all living organisms

Paris expressed regret

Pigs are wise they know what awaits them
Quality-control inspectors from the European Union
inspect Polish dairy farms and slaughterhouses
an Englishman and a Dutchman
went out for breakfast
and ate tongues in gelatin
"no comment" they said
at 6:30 p.m. the inspectors
ate pastrami
(spiced beef shank)
chuck roast and pork loin with plums

the European Union Inspectors
also noted a hole in the roof and a cockroach
they left the Meat Processing Plant
"no comment" they said to reporters

a swine plague in tulip country

in Holland the number of infection hot spots
grew to 133 hence the government
turned to the European Union
for help in slaughtering 5 million units of livestock
likewise in Spain where
20 mass mortality sites were noted
10 thousand pigs were slaughtered
and 132 thousand more hogs
and 60 thousand piglets will have to face it soon
the Swine Plague is an infectious disease afflicting pigs
the April tally of the Polish Bureau of Statistics showed
that we have in excess of 17.9 million pigs in Poland
9% less than in 1996
around the same time of year . . .

Paris expressed regret

on one of the farms in Kent county
cows responded to being milked
with fear and trembling
they started to spin and kneel
similar incidents are happening in barns all over
cows begin to dance double over with laughter
get hysterical fall down play blindman's bluff
there is a suspicion that the virus
is spread from pregnant
mother-cows to unborn
baby-calves
the British minister grins
like a madman
the French minister of agriculture
Philippe Vasseur warned yesterday—
"even if in countries such as France,
Italy, Spain, or Germany
scientists refrained from violating ethical principles,
somewhere someone could, nonetheless,
rear an eight-legged sheep
or a six-legged chicken"

Rosie looks like a normal cow
but Rosie of Glasgow is not a normal cow
Rosie is the first cow
to give human milk (or rather a woman's milk)
scientists injected her with human genes
now Rosie's milk
contains the protein alpha-lactalbumin,
found elsewhere only
in breast milk
the cows on TV are laughing
Polly the cloned sheep
with an added human gene
is the latest achievement of British scientists who
recently cloned Dolly
the goal of the experiment
was to breed a sheep
that could give milk
enriched by human protein

Hello Polly! Hello Dolly!

Doctors warn
against using live cell cultures
for which serum is often extracted
from the glands of sheep
sheep embryos and newborns have been lobotomized
to make facial masks for the mugs
of millionaires whores and gangsters

the germ is unpredictable

Laboratory goats and mice
fed meal from the brains of infected cows and sheep
came down with BSE
In 1976 Daniel Gajdusek received the Nobel Prize
for a discovery in this area
Many people already carry the
pathogens inside them
but the British are still exporting to Europe.
Knackeries

in the United Kingdom
can barely keep pace
with the torching of piles of corpses
from Creutzfeldt-Jakob disease
which can be passed on from parents to children
Another form of CJD
is called "Kuru"—the Laughing Death,
as many of its victims
grin madly in its final stages

Great Britain plays *"blinde Kuh"*
or blindman's bluff with the European Union

mad cows ruminate
in many European countries
in the United States Canada
Argentina Israel in Oman
and also in the Falkland Islands

Unde malum?

Where does evil come from?
what do you mean "where"

from a human being
always a human being
and only a human being

a human being is a work-related
accident
of nature
an error

if humankind
disentangles
itself
from flora and fauna

the earth will regain
its beauty and lustre

nature its purity
and innocence

human beings are the only beings
who use words
which can serve as tools of crime

words that lie
wound infect

evil does not come from an absence
or out of nothingness

evil comes from a human being
and only a human being

we differ in thought—as Kant said—
and for that matter in being
from pure Nature

From

the professor's knife,

2001

the professor's knife

I

TRAINS

a freight train
cattle cars
in a very long line

goes over fields and forests
green meadows
grasses and wild herbs
so quietly the buzzing of bees can be heard
it passes through clouds
golden buttercups
marsh marigolds bluebells
forget-me-nots
Vergissmeinnicht

this train
will not leave
my memory

a pen rusts

flies away turning beautiful in the light
of awakened spring

Robigus nearly unknown
the demon of rust—from the second tier of gods
consumes tracks and rails
steam engines

the pen rusts
ascends glides soars
over the earth like a lark
a rusty
stain on a blue sky
crumbles
falls to earth

flies
south

Robigus
who in ancient times
digested metals
—though he did not touch gold—
consumes keys
and locks
swords plowshares knives
guillotine blades axes

rails that run
parallel
without ever converging

a young woman
flag in hand
issues signals
and disappears
into oblivion

toward the end of the war
a gold train left Hungary
for parts unknown
"gold"? or so it was called
by American officers
mixed up in all this
they knew nothing
they heard nothing
they are dying off anyway

gold trains amber rooms
sunken continents
Noah's ark
maybe my Hungarian friends
have heard something about this train
maybe the *Kursbuch* survived
the last train schedule
from besieged Budapest

I'm standing in the last car
Inter Regnum—of the train
to Berlin
and I hear a child beside me
cry out
"See? The oak tree is running away!
Into the forest . . . "
a cart carries children away
I open my book
to a Norwid poem
and build
a bridge
linking the past
to the future

"The past is today
only a bit further away . . .
Beyond the wheels is a village
Not just anything, anywhere
Where no one has ever been"

freight trains
cattle cars
the color of liver and blood
in a long line
loaded with banal Evil
banal fear
despair
banal children women
girls
in the blush of youth

do you hear the cry
for one sip
for one sip of water
all of humanity cries
for but one sip
of banal water

I build a bridge
linking the past
to the future

the rails run
parallel
trains fly by
like blackbirds

ending their flight
in a fiery oven
from which
no singing rises
to the empty heavens
the train reaches
its destination
becomes
a monument

over fields meadows and forests
over hill and valley
it speeds ever more quietly
train of stone
perched
over the abyss
if brought to life by
the hateful cries
of racists nationalists
fundamentalists
it will fall like an avalanche
on humanity
not on "humanity"!

on a human being

II

THE EGG OF COLUMBUS

after all these years I'm sitting with Mieczysław
having breakfast
the twentieth century is ending

I slice bread on a cutting board
spread butter on it
add a pinch of salt

"Tadeusz, you eat too much bread . . . "

I smile I like bread
"you know"—I say—
"a slice of fresh bread
a slice, a heel
buttered
or with bacon bits in lard
with a dash of ground pepper"

Mieczysław rolls his eyes

I take a bite of crust
I know! salt isn't healthy
bread isn't healthy
(white bread!)
and sugar! that's death . . .

do you remember "sugar makes you strong"?!
that was probably a Wańkowicz slogan

Wańkowicz . . . Wańkowicz
we were "a superpower" then
but sugar no longer makes you strong

would you like a soft-boiled egg?
Mieczysław asks
eating
an egg for breakfast gets you off to a good start

Mieczysław is standing by the stove

Tadeusz! Don't talk to me
when I'm boiling an egg

because . . .

well . . . because . . . once again I forgot
how long it's been boiling

don't you have a watch or a clock or
a timepiece after all we are entering
the twenty-first century supermarkets internets
all kinds of eggtimers egg timers (?)
I'm never sure which
in modern households
in Germany
they have all kinds of gadgets clocks
they all ring beep or sound alarms!
they have these clever contraptions
where you can boil a whole egg
without the shell
in the microwave or perhaps
the shortwave I know nothing
about it Mieczysław, soon we will be eating
virtual eggs without the yolk
because the yolk isn't healthy
maybe not us but our grandchildren

Tadeusz! try to understand that boiling
an egg requires attention . . .
concentration even
it'll probably come out hard-boiled

Germans Germans they're so technological
high-tech eggs
techno and metal
music is not for us

and?!
and what?
what do you mean and what
how's the egg
we'll see
You taught
me how to crack an egg
I've always tapped the shell with a spoon

but you in one decisive
move use a knife
to cut off the top
of course with the egg in its holder
you don't muck up the spoon or your nails

how's yours?

mine's good
not too hard not too soft

but what were you doing . . . I saw
you poke a hole in the egg before you plopped it
in the water
what did you poke it with . . . a needle?
I'd never seen that trick
till today . . .
it figures! mine is hard-boiled

aren't you using too much salt

well . . . you know a soft-boiled egg
without salt and pepper . . .
there are certain principles . . . and as for
the boiling time my aunt had
a solution: say three hail marys
for a soft-boiled egg

but that is no solution for atheists

and this is an atheist speaking?

what atheist . . . have you ever seen
a real atheist or nihilist in Poland?

there have been freethinkers atheists
materialists communists activists
marxists and even trotskyists
so yes

so what? . . . they were in such a hurry
to join the pilgrimage
of the cultural and artistic elite
from Warsaw to Częstochowa
it's always been that way
everyone with his own Jew or priest
inside everyone there lurks a heroic monk Robak
Jankiel or Konrad Wallenrod

how does Konrad Wallenrod fit in?

I don't mean to scare you but you went a bit overboard with the salt

you know my memory is not what it used to be
listen if my life depended on it
I would not be able to recall
how it was with Columbus's egg
Columbus stood an egg on its end? how was he able
to balance it on a table on its end
I need to look it up in Kopaliński

you have your way and I have mine

scrambled eggs with sausage or bacon
is out of the question at this point

I recall now what Norwid said
at the Matejko exhibit in Paris
in 1876 (if I'm not mistaken) you know I've been immersed in
Norwid for two years now and I plan to write a short book
lessons on Norwid or lessons from Norwid
about the Matejko painting Norwid said
—I had missed this even though
I know practically everything about the painter—
he called it "our national scrambled eggs"
he was talking about "Sigismundus' Bell"
I don't know where the painting is now
Palais de l'Industrie (in 1873)
Our national scrambled eggs! between you and me
neither Europe nor America knows

what true scrambled eggs are like
that's right . . . how is the Norwid coming along
it's not coming along . . . to tell you the truth it's moving at a snail's pace
Art is like a banner on the tower of human works

he's incredible

III

SHADOWS

in the afternoon we visited
Hania's grave
Hania passed away five years ago
leaving Mieczysław alone

Robigus the demon of rust
coats the past in rust
covers the words eyes
and smiles
of the dead
the pen

we continue on
to the grave of Przyboś's wife Bronia
daughters and grandchildren
from Paris New York
attended the funeral

Przyboś wanted the elder one
to become a gardener a fruit grower
perhaps he dreamt that in his old age
he would have his very own apple tree
and would write
avant-garde poems
in the shade of the apple tree

in the shade of a tree

that he would continue his thing—
Kochanowski's thing

but
the metropolis the masses the machine
brought an unwelcome surprise
to the avant-garde poets
these things turned into a trap

the trains started moving

freight trains and cattle trains
loaded with banal evil
started to move from east
west
south and north

freight cars
loaded with banal fear
banal despair

to this very day banal tears
roll down
the faces of old women
after the war miraculous paintings wept
and living women
wept

sculptures wept people wept

IV

THE DISCOVERY OF THE KNIFE

Mieczysław sent me a letter
in 1998
in answer to my question
where the knife came from

did he make it himself
did he find it
steal it
dig it out of the ground

(the Iron Age)
did it fall from the sky
(after all miracles do happen)

Mieczysław:
"I've been thinking further about my knife,
the one made out of a barrel hoop.
you had to carry it in the hem of a concentration camp uniform
since they'd confiscate things
and one could pay dearly . . .
So it served its purposes,
not just utilitarian
but far more subtle ones
(it would be worth talking about it sometime) . . . "

Robigus covers the iron knife
with rust
slowly devouring it

I first saw it
on the Professor's desk
sometime around the middle of the twentieth century

strange knife I thought

neither a letter opener
nor a potato peeler
neither a paring knife nor a carving knife

it lay amidst Matejko and Rodakowski
Kantor Jaremianka and Stern
sheets of paper
Alina Szapocznikow
Brzozowski (another Tadeusz)
and Nowosielski amidst
conference papers and index cards
"strange knife" I thought
I picked it up
and put it back where it was

Mieczysław went into the kitchen
to make some tea (and he makes really strong black tea
way too strong for me
I always dilute it with water)
another twenty years passed

"strange knife" I thought
it lay between a book on Cubism
and the last page of a review article
he must use it as a letter opener
in the concentration camp
he peeled potatoes with it
or used it for shaving

why yes—the Professor said—
vegetable peels could save you
from starving to death

his orderly desktop reflected
the state of his mind

you know Mieczysław I will write a poem
about this knife
years passed
our children went to school
grew up graduated

it was 1968 . . . 1969
man walked on the Moon
I don't remember the exact date
it was the infamous March
the March of "writers go write!"
but someone broke my pen . . .
I spent the night at Mieczysław's
he lived in the building of the academy
of fine arts
on Krakowskie Przedmieście
rainy evening police and special units
unmarked cars patrol cars nightsticks
long nightsticks in the fog
helmets riot shields

the next day I ran into
Przyboś in Zachęta
what is it these students want he asked
he seemed surprised startled
then he began to explain to me
Strzemiński's theory of the afterimage
"students . . . "
he said as if to himself

I returned home
over dinner Mieczysław's daughter Joanna asked me
"and what do we do now? . . . " but I got the sense
she knew better than her father or the Great Przyboś
better than I . . . what to do . . .
I answered "stay calm"
Joanna smiled . . . and left the room

Mieczysław was in the hospital on Szaserów St.
he came to from anaesthesia
I sat alone in his study
familiar paintings on the wall
Strumiłło Nowosielski Brzozowski
Mieczysław's self-portrait from the time of the German occupation

the knife lay on newspaper

at the airport I read the signs
writers go write Zionists go home
(or was it the other way around?) on returning home
to my native soil
these words left a certain . . . taste in my mouth . . .
(a taste? of what?)
Aleksander Małachowski
had asked me to grant a TV interview
I said that one small step
a human footprint on the Moon
would change the world and mankind . . . How naïve.

V

TRAINS STILL DEPART

only now from memory

for Oświęcim Auschwitz
Teresin Gross-Rosen Dachau
for Majdanek Treblinka
Sobibor
for history
Blind tracks
trains depart
from small stops
from giant railway stations
turned art museum
Hamburg Paris Berlin
here artists
assemble their installations
trains
steam engines rust
on decommissioned rail lines
Robigus covers in rust
the rails signal boxes switches
soccer fans and conscripts
trash train cars
celebrate the happiest day
of their lives—
leaving the army
others are taking the oath
kissing the flag
parents wives girlfriends cry
the band strikes up a march

but the other train
that I see
(before the eyes of my soul)
has rebelled
left the tracks
the rails the lights
the switches

it goes over the green meadows
over dirt roads and wild herbs
over moss
over water
over sky
over clouds
over the rainbow's arc

is this Treblinka
asks a young girl
in the blush of her youth
I remember
her lips
and eyes like a handful of violets
it is Rose from Radomsko . . .
"I called her Rose
because you had to call her something
so she would have a name"
I don't remember
her real name

the train goes
over pillows
of silver and green
moss
through forest glades and clearings
through groves
of the righteous and unrighteous

that's Alina, I think to myself

Alina the sculptor
the student of Xawery Dunikowski
in a cattle car
opens a window
leans out kisses the wind
closes a window scarred
by barbed wire
I'm sitting so close
that our shoulders touch

"there is something in my eye"
I bend forward
I have a clean handkerchief I say
pull up your eyelid please
we will do a little surgery
without an anaesthetic
she smiles through the tears
don't be afraid
I say
it's only a speck of dust

it's not the first time
that I've done this procedure
you're my latest guinea pig
(she doesn't know yet
that she will be experimented on)

that's it—I say—
the tears will take care of the rest
I wipe her eyes
here's the culprit
I show her a sharp black
sliver of coal

allow me to introduce myself
my name is Tadeusz
I'm Rose . . . Mom and I are going
from Teresin to Treblinka
Mom is in the dining car
they split us up
her car is at the very end of the train

we will be getting off at Treblinka
you know I'm dying of hunger
seriously
I am so hungry
I could eat a horse
or a carrot
a turnip
a core of cabbage
and . . . where are you headed Sir? if I may ask

me? wherever! off to the woods
to pick mushrooms berries
get some fresh air

I am a Satyr
the girl laughs

now I can tell you a secret
I get off at the next stop
the place the unit is stationed is called
"tall trees"

VI

THE LAST CENTURY

I looked at the knife
it could have been used for cutting bread
a knife from the Iron Age
—I thought—from a death camp

The Iron Age
shame truth honesty fled
treason deceit fraud violence
took their place
and the criminal desire to own things
cunning man carved up the earth with borders
the earth which was common to all until then
just like the light
the sun the air
cruel iron came into the world
and something even more cruel than iron—gold . . .

the knife
made from a barrel hoop
a beer barrel or some other barrel
with a handle
so ingeniously
bent

Hania the Professor's wife has passed on

when the Professor sits with his eyes closed
in silence thinks writes
prepares a lecture
departs from scholarship
toward math and philosophy
or maybe logic and mysticism
recalls what he did
with that knife in the camp
sliced and apportioned the bread
saved every crumb
didn't peel potatoes
(nor throw out peels
since they could save someone from
starving to death)

years have passed—
we reckon that
between the two of us
we are 160 years old
the twentieth century has come to an end . . .

the Professor lives alone works cannot sleep
listens to music
I came to Ustroń
from Radomsko
from memory from out of the past

I came to Ustroń again
in July of 2000 from Wrocław and
Kraków by way of Wadowice
I wanted to see the hometown of the poet Jawień

I was moved I saw his mountains his clouds
the house he grew up in the school the simple church

the gate

Lasciate ogni speranza
Voi ch'entrate

abandon all hope
ye who enter here

the inscription at the entrance to the inferno
of Dante's *Divine Comedy*

courage!

beyond that gate
there is no hell

hell has been dismantled
by theologians
and deep psychologists

converted into allegory
for humanitarian and educational
reasons

courage!

beyond that gate
the same thing begins again

two drunken gravediggers
sit at the edge of a hole

they're drinking nonalcoholic beer
and munching on sausage
winking at us
they play soccer
with Adam's skull
under the cross

the hole awaits
tomorrow's corpse
the "stiff" is on its way

courage!

here we will await
the final judgment

water pools in the hole
cigarette butts are floating in it

courage!

beyond that gate
there will neither be history
nor goodness nor poetry

and what will there be
dear stranger?

there will be stones

stone
upon stone
stone upon stone
and on that stone
one more
stone

Ghost Ship

the days grow shorter
the sundial stands
hourless in the rain

the sanitarium emerges
from the clouds
like a vast ocean liner

columns of black trees
are dripping with water and moonlight

the sanitarium sails away
along with the November mist

rocking on the waters
windows dim one by one
plunging into darkness
into sleep

while below
underground
the devil's lit the old stove
in "Little Hell"

don't be afraid
it's only a café
a late-night spot

the saved and the condemned
their cheeks flush
lap up what is left of life

the fever rises
and everything whirls
in a dance of death
around woman's dark places

the ghost ship
runs aground

stick on water

A Kraków poem for Zosia and Jerzy Nowosielski

I

In my stormy youth
I flew over Kraków

after forty-five years
I'm back here again

I perch myself in the Planty Gardens
and then on the bridge

under the poplars amidst
shifting shadows

("the crown of my head
became a white bird")

ludicrous Anxiety
whether the house is
where it's always been

everything so unsettled
uncertain in this world
even the end of the world

I ring the bell I mount the stairs

my friends are already there
Jerzy in a blue smock
opens his arms
even his work wear
is dazzling to the eye
and from inside
I hear Zosia's
familiar voice

we speak about everything and nothing
even about the weather
we even speak of those things
whereof one cannot speak
*"Whereof one
cannot speak . . . "*
this fierce formula
put forth by Wittgenstein
was reversed by me
at just the right moment:
whereof one cannot speak
thereof one must speak

something well known to
women old men children and child poets

II

Why are you torturing yourself
try to write carefree
no rhyme or reason
lightly
effortlessly

don't make so much out of it

Zosia I
that is I
of course I try to write

light carefree
even with my left foot
but it's tethered to a stone

you have to forget yourself
you have to forget
that it's YOU who is writing

Write some doggerel
it will bring you joy
set you free
liberate you
open doors
to outlandish things
Jerzy says to me

Doggerel?
in a state of weightlessness
no one writes doggerel

Doggerel!
easy for you to say
you Painter

so! let's go into town
perhaps around the corner we will meet
a Guardian Angel

Jerzy you may see
but I do not see
your angel

we walk along the river
the blind leading the lame
we go and go

but Tadeusz Kantor is already gone
and Brzozowski too
Jarema and Filipowicz
Ewa Lassek
and Hania Porębska

I feel lighter and lighter

I sit at a table
a pen flees my hand
a feather drifts

on a sheet of paper
a dry black
stick

I write as if on water

February–March 1993

rain in Kraków

rain in Kraków
rain
falls on the Wawel dragon
on the bones of giants
on Kościuszko Mound
on the Mickiewicz Monument
on Podkowiński's *Ecstasy*
on Mr. Dulski
on the bugle call from the tower of St. Mary's Church

rain
rain in Kraków
falls on the white Skałka
on the green Błonia grasslands
on Marshal Piłsudski's coffin
beneath the silver bells
on gray infantry

clouds settle
blanketing Kraków
rain

rain falls
on the eyes of Wyspiański
on his blind stained glass

the timid eye of a clear blue sky
a thunderbolt from above

long-legged girls in platform shoes
fold up their bright umbrellas
it clears up
the sun
comes out
I wander around monasteries
looking for *The Dance of Death*

in the hotel room
I try to catch
a fleeting poem

Onto a sheet of paper
I pin a butterfly
a blue one
a blot of sky

rain rain rain
in Kraków
I'm reading Norwid
it's sweet to be asleep
sweeter still to be made of stone

good night dear friends
good night
poets dead and living
good night poetry

July 2000

From

gray area,

2 0 0 2

cobweb

four gray women
Need Poverty Worry Guilt
lie in wait far away

a person is born
grows up
starts a family
builds a home

these four phantoms
lie in wait
hidden in the foundation

they build
a second home for him
a labyrinth
in a blind alley

he lives loves
prays and works
fills the home with hope
tears laughter
and fright

the four gray women
play hide-and-seek
with him
they lurk in chests
closets bookcases

they feed on gloves dust
mothballs swampy ground
eat books
fade mousygray
in the icy moonlight
sit on paper flowers
the children clap their hands

trying to kill a clothes moth and some other moth
but the moths turn into silence
silence into music

the four gray women lie in wait

the person invites
other people
to christenings funerals
weddings and wakes
silver and golden anniversaries
uninvited
through the keyhole
enter the four gray women

first to appear is Guilt
behind her looms Worry
slowly Need grows
Poverty bares her teeth

the home turns into a cobweb

voices groans
gnashing of teeth
and rattling can be heard

awakened gods
drive off
the pesky humans
and yawn

gray area

"What makes gray a neutral color?
Is it something physiological, or logical?"
"Grayness is situated between two extremes (black and white)"
—Wittgenstein, Remarks on Color

my gray area
increasingly includes poetry

here white is not absolute white
black is not absolute black
the edges of these noncolors
touch

Wittgenstein's question is answered by Kępiński

"The world of depression is a monochromatic world
dominated by grayness or total darkness

in the drab grayness of depression many things may look
different than in normal light"

black and white flowers
grew only in Norwid's poetry
Mickiewicz and Słowacki
were colorists

the world we live in
is a variegated vertigo
but I don't live in that world
I was only rudely awakened
can one be awakened politely

I see
in the green grass
an orange cat
hunting a gray mouse

the artist Get
tells me he cannot see colors

he can tell them apart by the labels
on the tubes and cans

they tell him which one is which
yellow red blue

but his palette is gray

he sees a gray cat
in the gray grass
hunting a gray mouse

he has impaired vision
(it's not that he suffers from depression)
maybe he feigns it
to provoke his students
liven up our discussions

we go on talking about
Remarks on Color
W. talks of a red circle
a red square a green circle

I say to G. it only seems
that the square is filled
with red or green
the square is square
not red or green
according to Lichtenberg only
a handful have ever seen pure white

drawing may be the purest
art form
it is filled
with pure emptiness

that's why by its very nature
a drawing is
closer to the absolute
than a Renoir painting

the Germans say
weiße rose and *rote rose*
to someone who doesn't know German
a rose
is neither *rote* nor *weiße*
it's just a rose
but to someone who has never heard the word
"rose" what he holds in his hand
is a flower or a pipe

regression into the primordial soup *(die Ursuppe)*

in the beginning
was a thick soup where
under the influence of light (and heat)

life was born

out of the soup came a creature
or rather something
that turned into yeast
into a chimp
some time later a god appeared
and created a human being
man and woman
sun kitten and tick

man invented the wheel
and wrote *Faust*

started printing
paper money
various things came into being

donuts Fat Tuesday
Platonic love pedophilia
Poetry Day (sic!)
Arthritis Awareness Day (sic!)
Day of the Sick—today's the day
finally I too came into the world
in the year 1921 and suddenly . . .
atchoo! time passes I am old and lose my glasses
I forgot there was
history Caesar Hitler Mata Hari
Stalin capitalism communism
Einstein Picasso Al Capone
Alka-Seltzer Al Qaeda

in my eighty years
I have noticed that "everything"
turns into a strange soup
—but the soup of death not life
I drown in the soup of death
I cry out in English
help me help me
(no one understands Polish anymore)

I grasp at straws
(someone else grabbed the bull by the horns)

a long long time ago
Józef Wittlin
the Saint Francis of Polish poetry
wrote a paean to a spoonful of soup
but I forget what kind of soup
then all of a sudden my wife
steps out of the kitchen

she grows more beautiful by the day
"are you going to have supper with me?"
"I've eaten already" she says

if I were King Solomon
I would have written for you

the song of songs
but even Solomon could not
squeeze blood from
a stone let alone a poet
from Radomsko!
(not Florence nor Paris
but mere
Radomsko . . .) Radomka
my hometown rivulet
or maybe rivulit or rivulett
rivulette? Having
turned eighty I am no longer
bound by spelling rules
. . . Tadeusz my dear
why go to such effort?

in my old age I've lived to see a site
a web a chat room thread
a menu a mouse
I look at the big dipper
above me
and I don't know what to make of it
I look at the little dipper
dipper dipper time is ticking

Goethe's grandson was great
what did he say?
. . . *I stand before the Capitol*
and do not know what I should do

while Grandpa had to write
Dichtung und Wahrheit
and add an entire *Italian Journey*

bravo! bravo! for the grandson
time to return to the primordial soup
brothers in poetry (and sisters too)
let's go back to the anal phase
there you have the origin of
all the arts

fine and ugly
tertium non datur? is there no other way?
well! *datur datur* there is there is
tertium is being born
before our very eyes

* * *

> *"It's over and done with [. . .]*
> *It would be best to go insane."*
> —*Tadeusz Konwicki,* Twilight

And once again
the past begins

You're right Tadeusz
it would be best to go insane
but our generation never quite goes insane
we keep our eyes open
to the very end

we don't need to be blindfolded
we have no need for the sundry paradises
of various faiths sects religions

backs broken
we crawl on

yes Tadeusz as we near the end
we have to relive everything
from the beginning
you know that as well as I
at times we whisper
all people will be brothers
in life's labyrinth
we encounter
faces of friends turned inside out

nameless
enemies

do you hear me
let me share with you a memory of the past
once again I'm running away
from a phantom who
cloaked in a swatch of sky
stands in a green meadow
and speaks to me in an unfamiliar tongue
I am the lord thy god
who led thee out of the house of bondage

everything starts from the beginning

once again Mr. Turski
my choir teacher
looks at me with the beautiful
sweet eyes
of Omar Sharif

and I sing
"the apple tree's in bloom (. . .)
red apples it will bear"
I know I'm out of tune
but Mr. Turski has been smiling
at me since 1930
and I get an A
Mr. Turski in a strange
fragrant cloud
exotic and mysterious
for a grade school teacher
in a provincial town
between Częstochowa and Piotrków Trybunalski
smiles
and takes his secret
to the grave

when will the past
finally end

Alarm Clock

it's hard
to be the shepherd of the dead

time and again
the living ask me
to write "something" "a tidbit"
about someone who has died
departed passed on rests
in peace

and I am the one who is still living writing
living and writing yet again

let the dead bury their own dead

I listen to the ticking of the clock
it's an old alarm clock
made in China
(note: Shanghai, China)
back in the time of the Great Helmsman
who let a hundred flowers bloom
and called on a hundred schools of art
to compete
and then came the Cultural Revolution

my alarm clock is like a tractor
you need to "wind it with a crank"
(do you remember the saying
of the Polish philistines the pseudointellectuals the agrarian accountants
"give shit to a peasant not a watch
or else he'll wind it with a crank"
the peasants have forgotten . . . but "the poet remembers")
I wind it like Gerwazy
it wakes me at five
you can count on it
like the old Chinese man who nodded his head
in the display window of a colonial goods store

above a tea canister
the alarm clock wakes me
a few times a year
reminding me that
I need to go somewhere fly somewhere
north south
east west
or that I need to get up at the break of dawn
and finish a "poem"
hundert Blumen blühen
(I bought the little red book
of chairman Mao
in Munich
with a foreword by Lin Biao)

I the poet—the shepherd of life
have now become the shepherd of the dead

I have been grazing far too long
in the meadows of your graveyards
go away leave me
in peace

this is a matter for the living

Too Bad

I never finished
Paradise mea culpa
I got bored in *Purgatory*
mea culpa
only *Hell*
did I read with flushed cheeks
mea maxima culpa

Ezra Pound
read not only all of

Dante and Confucius
but also the poet from Predappio
(la Clara a Milano!)
whom he adored

Pound was a lunatic a genius
and a martyr
His most prized student
Possum
wrote lovely poems about cats
wore tasteful ties
chose his words more carefully
than his master
and won a Nobel Prize for it

Pound
was right
not to like
capitalists and usurers

he wanted to drive the merchants
out of the temple
they put him in a
straitjacket
he walks around Parnassus
in it
where he talks to the admirer of
Dante Ariosto Schiller
Klopstock Platen
Waiblinger . . .
to the poet composer leader
translator and the author of the poem
"Die Worte vom Brot"
to Benito Mussolini himself!
(you deserved it! you silly poet you)

P.S.
too bad Pound had not yet read
Mein Kampf
before he started to praise
the Führer

why do I write?

sometimes "life" obscures
That
which is greater than life

sometimes mountains obscure
That
which is beyond the mountains
therefore we need to move mountains
but I do not have all the necessary
technology
nor the strength
nor the faith
to move mountains
therefore you will
never
see It
I know
therefore
I write

Escape of the Two Piglets
(from the death camp—the slaughterhouse)

today someone told me
an amusing
and curious story . . . it happened
on an island where an English tribe
clones sheep where cow's
milk has the nutritional properties of human milk
where people go mad
along with dogs
that have eaten meal made from sheep's brains

two piglets escaped from the slaughterhouse
dug a tunnel under the fence
fled through field and grove
swam across a stream and a river

as guards dogs helicopters
searched high and low
a flock of cloned sheep
bleated in the meadow

till the fugitives were caught at last

this time "humanity" came to the rescue
moved by the plight
of god's creatures
instead of turning the piglets
into ham and spam
the government awarded them a pension
and sentenced them to life
the heir to the throne himself
granted them his protection
in the wake of this news
my waning faith in the prince
returned to me
reborn

P.S.
three days later I read
that the lives of the piglets may still be in danger
for the slaughterhouse owner has sued
he wants to get them back
turn them into bacon sausages
hocks spareribs and ham
(the law is on his side . . . property rights . . .
in murky Albion the law
is a sacred thing) . . .
how the story of the piglets ends I don't know
the century has turned the page
it's now the Harry Potter age

Sobbing Superpower
(Saturday, January 20, 2001)

I'm reading Norwid

Over the mobile plains of the sea
I send you a song like a seagull, John

Long will she fly to the land of the free
Doubting she will find it so

I'm in Konstancin at a writer's retreat
talking with Ryszard Kapuściński
about Franek Gil
about globalization
we're drinking wine
I speak of population growth
he speaks of water shortages
not oil but water
not water
but lack of water will be the cause
of wars Ryszard says
blood will be spilled over water
not over homeland honor or god

it's gotten late

I hear that in far off
Washington it's sleeting
it's cold, foul weather
the new, 43rd president of the Superpower
is being sworn in
21-gun salute at the Capitol

The Superpower is sentimental
touchy-feely compassionate
(*"mitfühlender Konservativismus"*)
quick to tears

"compassionate conservative"
hand on Bible
the son of the 41st president

Abraham Lincoln looks on and listens

not even the downpour could
hide Bush's tears
the Superpower sobbed

The president's wife Laura wept
his twin daughters wept
the president's parents wept
former president George Bush
and his wife—Grandma Barbara
Gore's electorate wept
those who made sloppy holes
in the ballot cards
the holes that had to be counted over
the outgoing president
Bill Clinton wept his wife Hillary wept
(she wept but took the chairs
and loveseat wept but took the table
and curtains and who knows what else
. . . though she did give them back) their daughter
Chelsea wept Madeline
in a mini skirt a rose at her bosom
kept drying her eyes Bronek
wept too (but for different reasons)
the former
national security advisor
Sandy Berger
"kept reaching for his hankie"
the sky wept
vice president
Dick Cheney wept
as the 43rd president sheltered him from the rain
with his own coat
("compassionate conservative")
flipping up his collar
(to protect his own neck from the rain)

An obscure young intern wept
as did her mother who was left
with a soiled dress
in the closet
"My dear sweet child . . . "
what have you done?!
then there was a ball
made up of a hundred balls
and what a ball it was

for gentlemen the dress code was tails
and cowboy boots
or a tux
and cowboy boots

top hat or cowboy hat and cowboy boots

then there was a banquet
sixty-six hundred pounds of beef were consumed
(the old world would feel it in a few years
or even a few days)
fifty-five hundred pounds of ham
(also not a good omen)
and sixty thousand jumbo shrimp

the former president
bid the nation farewell yet again
again he apologized to the prosecutor and the nation
for lying about putting his finger where
it didn't belong
the finger for pushing the nuke button
don't catch your finger in the door!
promised to give back the chairs
and took off

the sky wept the earth wept
land and sea trembled
diplomats and generals
were blowing their noses

(the cardinals smiled shyly)

I too wept
reading the papers
then I listened to the radio
and laughed through the tears

From

exit,

2004

* * *

white is neither sad
nor glad
it's just white

I tell it
and tell it
it's white

but white does not listen
it is deaf
and dumb

it's just right

and getting
whiter and whiter
with time

philosopher's stone

we need to put
this poem to sleep

before it starts
philosophizing
before it starts

fishing
for compliments

called to life
in a moment of forgetting

sensitive to words
glances
it looks to
a philosopher's
stone for help
o passerby hasten your step
do not lift up the stone

there a blank verse
naked
turns
to ashes

2002–2003

words

words have been used up
chewed up like chewing gum
by lovely young mouths
and turned into a white
bubble

weakened by politicians
they serve to whiten
teeth
to cleanse the oral
cavity

when I was a child
a word
could heal wounds
could be given
to a loved one

now weakened
wrapped in newspaper words

still poison still stink
still inflict wounds

hidden in heads
hidden in hearts
hidden under dresses
of young women
hidden in holy books
they explode
and kill

2004

avalanche

an avalanche fell upon our heads
made of granite gravel granules

one might say that poets
have stoned poetry to death
with words

only the stuttering
Demosthenes put
stones to good use
he churned them
inside his mouth
until they drew blood
and became one of the greatest
orators
in the world

P.S.
when I first set out
I too stumbled over a stone

my old Guardian Angel

an avalanche of angels
brought on by
inspired poets
painters priests
and American
film directors
is far more silly for heaven's sake
than the one brought on by
the Romantic poets

the products of
the dream works
"holy wood"
are sugar-sweet white
like the cotton candy
kids
love

my Guardian Angel who
is eighty-three now
and remembers all
my little sins
came to me frightened
and started to
tell me that he is being molested
by peddlers
pedophiles pederasts
from network Television
public Television and the evangelical channel
who want him to endorse
angel milk the one with little wings
break-dance with senior citizens
sell
menstrual pads with wings
or without wings

they gave him
a gold watch with no time
a depilator a vibrator
a lawnmower a cell phone
a free trip to Babylon

another dumbbell
offered him
the post of Angel of Europe
and guardian angel of the Euro

my good old Guardian Angel
buried his face in his wings
and sobbed
"don't cry" I said—
Angel of God my guardian dear
to whom God's love entrusts me here
ever this day be at my side
to light and guard to rule and guide

and so arrived my
Guardian Devil
black wings
sprouting from his heels

and so began the fight
over my soul
Guardian Angel and Guardian Devil

golden thoughts against a dark background

ever since I woke up
I've been having dark thoughts

dark thoughts?

maybe you could try to describe
their form their content

how do you know they are dark

maybe they are square
red
or golden

that's right!

golden thoughts

golden scales in the dead sea
of tired language

for example these from Gogol
"nothing soothes
like history"
or
"laughter is no laughing matter"

and one more thought
that should be pondered
by young people
and those in "the prime of life"

"the world would be far worse off
without old people"

P.S.
there would be no one
to give up your seat for on the bus
what good is life
without good deeds

a fairy tale

my legs fell asleep
I woke up
from a long
uncomfortable
dream

in a pure world

in a newly
born light
in Bethlehem or perhaps
some other mean city

where no one murdered
children
or cats
Jews or Palestinians
water trees
or air

where there was neither past
nor future

I held the hands of
Mom and Dad
the Lord God that is

and I felt so good
as if
I didn't exist

Christmas 2002

a finger to the lips

the lips of truth
are pressed tight

a finger to the lips
tells us
the time has come

for silence

no one will answer
the question
what is truth

the one who knew
the one who was the truth
is gone

the last conversation

instead of responding
to my question
you held a finger to your lips

Jerzy said

is this a sign
that you do not want to
that you cannot answer

this is my answer
to your question
"what is the meaning of life
if I must die?"

by holding a finger to my lips
I answered you in thought
"life only has meaning
because we must die"

eternal life
life without end
is being without meaning
light without shadow
echo without voice

heart rises to throat

in 1945
in October
I left the resistance

and could breathe again

word by word
I was regaining speech

it seemed to me
that "Everything" was falling
into place
not just in my head
but in the world
at home in my country

with Przyboś I searched for
a place on earth
with Staff I began
rebuilding from
the smoke rising from the chimneys
with Kotarbiński
I voted "three times yes"

I was a student in Ingarden's
seminar
an introduction to epistemology
Hume helped me
order my thoughts

the referendum was rigged

the rebuilding of the temple
progressed according
to plans and dreams
God left me alone
do as you wish you are a grown-up
he said
don't hold me by the hand
don't turn to me
with every trifle
I have two billion people to take care of
soon I will have ten billion
I helped you in 1935
to solve those equations
with one variable God spoke
from a burning bush
that turned to ashes

the twenty-first-century was stealing in like a thief

my head
was scattered to the four corners of the globe
on the wall I saw
an inscription Mane Tekel Fares
in Babylon a knife to a human throat

eternal return . . .

Nietzsche is back in vogue
returning to Germany (and Poland)
in a roundabout way
via Paris
in the guise of a French philosopher
of Rumanian extraction

Zarathustra of Naumburg
part Polish nobleman
part Übermensch

asks himself
his mother
sister

why am I so bright
brave unique crucified

best not think about it
his mother counsels
tend to your Greeks
or write something

His sister "liebes Lama"
fresh back from South America
is a bit concerned but still proud
that her brother has straight posture
and the looks of a soldier (*almost*)
"*his stomach and intestines still in good order*"

Fritz went down to the train station
bearing flowers but without the large saber
he had taken to the photographer
and to war (in his role as a medic)

then as befits an eagle
he searched for nests on the peaks

of Genoa and thereabouts
"sono contento"
he wrote home

the kindhearted people of Genoa
call him "il piccolo santo," the little saint
"il santo"
has regrettably abandoned
the idea of eternal return
he makes himself risotto and macaroni
(without onion or garlic)
artichokes with eggs and fresh tomatoes
diet is the essence of philosophy
what you eat you excrete
as thought
"the eternal return"

he asked his mother what
"ordinary" "common folk" eat
what our poor eat

"lonely Nietzsche"
did not know the "common folk"
he had little contact with the poor

our people
my dear Fritz
eat potatoes from dawn till dusk
fatty meat
pork
chase it with Schnapps
drink the weak hogwash
they call coffee

oh, Mother!
so their diet is an endless cycle of beef
potatoes weak coffee
and sauerkraut?

How little I know of the folk
I've always eaten alone

it's the leaders of the Social Democratic Party
who are to blame for everything
Mother . . .
a man should
be bred to be a soldier
a woman to be a soldier's wife

with tears in his eyes
he abandoned the idea
of eternal return
he understood
that eternal return to Naumburg
is nothing thrilling

and the climate just won't do
and the food and the neighbors
and his sister Lama and his mom
even though they're dear . . .
and the aunties!
can an eagle have aunties?
even if they are kind and tender

"yonder lies the sea
pale and glittering
it cannot speak"

philosophers

"The essence of truth
is freedom"
wrote Martin Heidegger
in 1930
he later joined
Hitler's party
"the Jumping Jack of the Nazis"
or so he was called by
Karl Jaspers
the just among philosophers

but he too was wrong
when he told Hannah Arendt
frightened by Hitler's victory
"This whole thing is an operetta
I will not be a hero in an operetta"
H.A. emigrated . . .
Jaspers stayed . . .
and he and his
Jewish wife Gertrude
found out
that this was no operetta.

the crystal night reigned
over Germany and Europe
the starry sky was dimmed
the moral law died

From

so what it's a dream,

2006

so what it's a dream

I write on water

from a few sentences
from a few verses
I build an ark

to save something
from the flood
that catches us by surprise
washes us off of the earth's
surface
when full of joy
we turn our faces
to the Sun god
and to the God
who
"does not play dice"
we know Nothing
about fractures in the bowels
of old mother earth
we build towers
out of sand
build
at the edge
of life and death

our Mother earth
sky blue and rounded
cloaked in veils of clouds
filled with amniotic waters
of life
full of volcanic fire
between two white ice
caps green smelling of sap
slightly flattened
after the bloody periods of wars
after the orgasms

of revolution
drifts into dreams of

the Garden of Eden
the Olympian gods
the one in the highest
the earth breathes turns beautiful
gathers strength and rosy cheeks
breathes deeply
rests up after the creative evolution
just like a she-wolf
feeds human cubs
abandoned by gods
forgetful
of their duties

My ark settles slowly
on the shallow waters of words dreams

a crowd builds
awaits a white dove
fireworks and balloons
awaits with curiosity
the human survivors
animals and trees
moles and birds of paradise

But no one emerges
from the ark

A drunken builder
sleeps amidst naked bodies
which decompose and stink

My name is Kanawaga
my name is Tsunami
a young girl giggles
shows the tattoos
on her butt on her belly
snooping cameras rove

over pubic mounds
full of seaweed and pearls
slide over labia
over mouths
full of sand and seashells

carrion stinks
providence scales on her eyes
watches over us
colorful bags with the remains of
the drowned lie scattered all over
or arranged in trucks
refrigerators mass graves
ditches meat lockers
the waters had not yet receded
when tourists appeared on beaches
pretty girls
wearing T-shirts that said

Let's Tsunami
Tsunami With Me

all kinds of gadgets are being sold
toys and stuffed animals
pictures of decomposing
bodies carcasses of animals of people
children being bought
being sold
to brothels

the Tsunami is a colorful
media-friendly sight on the surface
of infinity
Snooping cameras dig through corpses
lenses penetrating defenseless dead bodies
journalists and photographers
carry off in their claws
fragments scraps and pieces
of human flesh watches
heads arms rings hands

earrings entrails notebooks cell phones
slowly "everything"
returns to normal
Tourists do not cancel
prepaid vacations

it's a good show it boosts adrenaline
breaks ratings records

I write on water
I write on sand
out of a handful of salvaged words
out of a few sentences simple
like the carpenter's speech
out of a few naked verses
I build an ark
to save something
from the flood
that catches us by surprise
in broad daylight
or in the dead of night
washes us off of the earth's surface

I am building my ark
a drunken boat
paper ship
under red
black sails

So what it's a dream

Wrocław 2004–2005

farewell to Raskolnikov

The waiter pretended to be wiping off the table

I wanted to be a Napoléon
Raskolnikov said casually
but all I did was kill a louse

I decided to act
boldly with flair
to pave the way
to being somebody

the air in the luncheonette
was thick and rancid

I was sitting with a former law student
a glass of cloudy tea
on our table
on a plate was a stale
squashed napoleon
greenish cream oozed from the pastry
like dried-up pus
sprinkled with powdered sugar

I forgot about Raskolnikov
he forgot about me
we all have our own concerns

a black fly from out of nowhere
animated Raskolnikov
he set his tea aside
and started swatting with the newspaper
his article was in

I knew that he was dying
to show me
or even read aloud his essay
the first publication of a young writer

and scholar in a hazy
far-off future

I remember this strange special
feeling I now shared
with Raskolnikov the exaltation
my name in print!
youth has its privileges

Forgive me but it was ridiculous
of course you wanted to act
with flair hence an axe
not a fingernail
for if Napoléon had wanted
to kill a louse, he would have used his fingernail
or that of one of his marshalls

you mock me he said
I know the whole thing was
amateurish and shabby
to tell you the truth I did it
out of boredom
I killed in my sleep
I killed a louse in my sleep
but the axe was real
I fired a cannon
at a louse
that's the kind of Schiller I am
Raskolnikov fell into thought
then got up and left
without shaking hands
I was left alone with the napoleon
paid for the tea
and left

Raskolnikov
was still standing in front of the luncheonette
which way are you headed I asked
"me? the other way" he said
casually shrugging his shoulders

he walked with his head down
turned right on Sienna Street
soon after
I heard laughter and yelling
whistling and the tinkling of bells

I looked back

Raskolnikov was kneeling in the middle of the road
in a puddle of mud and snow
and horse "chestnuts"
the new top hat Sonya bought for him
he left on the cobblestone

he kissed the pavement three times made the sign of the cross
then crossed himself . . . applause followed
some rascal knelt alongside Raskolnikov

I tried to help him up but he pushed me away
gently and rose from his knees
took me by the arm
and said confidentially
"here one must be
as inconspicuous as possible . . .
Details, details
above all
It's always the details that
give you away . . . "
you go right and I go left
or the other way around . . . *adieu*
mon plaisir . . . till we meet again!

We never did meet again

2004–2005

Ezra Pound
one of the Church Fathers of poetry
hated
gold
bankers the stock market usury
and he was dead right

but

when I think of him
I am torn

this blinded Tiresias
saw clearly
he was punished
because he saw the naked truth
The Living God
of the capitalist world
The Golden Calf
fed cannon fodder
smeared with blood
of the best young
chosen
Sons

Ezra Pound cursed trusts
arms manufacturers the firms of
Krupp Zaharoff Schneider-Creusot
and other merchants of death
that half-baked economist
champion of Mussolini and Hitler
that son of a bitch Ezra Pound
Eliot's Master *il miglior fabbro*
was at times a poet of genius
also a great writer was
that son of a bitch Céline
Merlin

or so he was called in *Le
Parisien* by Ernst Jünger
the decorated veteran the champion
of the storm of steel
Merlin lectured the Germans
on how to handle the Jews

Merlin
revived French prose
expressed his astonishment that
we do not hang Jews
that we don't shoot Jews
"if I had a bayonet
I would know what to do with it"

Ezra Pound and Céline
loved cats and dictators
the smell of flowers and herbs
they helped the poor

despite all shortcomings
breaches of faith betrayals
they had one strong suit
they lacked "good taste"

they betrayed themselves they betrayed me
a younger apprentice
in the poetic trade

"There died a myriad
And of the best among them
For an old bitch gone in the teeth
For a botched civilization"

Eliot's Master a better maker
cursed the usurers
disparaged Krupp Zaharoff
Thyssen Schneider-Creusot
blasted oilmen
bankers arms manufacturers

Ernst Jünger and Merlin
met in Paris salons
where Cocteau read
his new play
constantly resounding *file file file*
go round round and round

Merlin lectured the Germans
on how to handle
Jews—Jünger recalls
"Death is always by my side"
he said staring into the distance
while Madame B. served
tea in a salon full of collaborators

Ezra Pound helped impoverished
poets Céline provided medical assistance to
the poor and homeless
both loved cats and dictators

These two scoundrels (and that third one)
betrayed themselves betrayed me
a younger apprentice
in the poetic trade

"Midway upon the journey of our life
I found myself within a forest dark,
For the straightforward pathway had been lost."
I was "searching for a teacher and a Master"
I read *Leaves of Grass*
by Walt Whitman I wrote *The Plains*
it was 1953 it was my dream that someday someone
would say about me
"*ei dice cose e voi dite parole—*
he says things and you say words"
long and convoluted was my path
at the end of it stood Ezra Pound

I heard
his mad barking

when he stopped barking
I listened to the silence
and heard the voice of a poet
the same man

"good poetry should be
as good and as clear
as good prose"
this one sentence from poetry
was more fertile than
the avant-garde tongue twisters
jester's bells
the dance of poetry in literary salons
between two slaughterhouses

"There died a myriad
And of the best among them
For an old bitch gone in the teeth
For a botched civilization"
said this church Father of poetry
prophet and traitor
vicious and virtuous

he was the first to give a kick in the ass
to a capitalist goldscheisser
the giant ass sitting on five continents
shitting gold and crude oil
into the pure waters of oceans
into the ether where the Word once dwelled
and from which the gods had evaported

they put an old
genius fool
into a cage
gave him an award
brought a lawsuit against him

then they let him go

he lived long and unhappily
a madman on paper
in the bosom of a botched civilization
and died in Venice

he descended into hell
"it was on the way"
and there he saw the shadows of traitors
submerged in ice

I cast a stone at him
sometimes I pull out that stone
from the pocket of a workman's jacket
in which I write poems
every day including holidays

I place it on my open palm
where the lines of life and death
blur

I look think weigh
put it back in my pocket

as a memento of
our Homeric battles
over the soul of a poet
the soul of poetry

it was not Circe who turned a poet
into a swine
it was Clio graver in hand
who was a Teacher
of Life and in her old age
became a Madame d'bordello and an aunt
of media revolutions
Ezra Pound
lacked "good taste"

but history and poetry
are not a cookbook

You don't do that to Kafka

Kafka's monument stands in Prague

of course it didn't stand up on its own
it was raised without being asked
whether it wants to stand there
and in what incarnation

the sculptor wrapped his work
tightly in babble
wagging his tongue
until the monument was left
speechless

as you can see
the monument consists
of an empty sportcoat
and baggy pants
this brass bag
is filled with the ghost
of the evil father

on his shoulders sits
an adult Franz—elegantly
dressed—in a fedora
and tightly creased
bronze pants

the son sits on the shoulders
of his giant Father
the evil Father

despite his tongue
very quick tongue
and moves straight out of a circus show
the sculptor
couldn't turn
a weak monument
into a work of art

in a Jewish cemetery in Prague
I saw
a stone monument
with Father and Mother lies
the famous
Son of whom they knew
so little . . .

From my Czech
translator Vlasta who met
Ottla's daughter Vera
I know that
the silk merchant Hermann K.
the son of a butcher was a good
and caring patriarch
a good husband
who loved his son
laughed at Max Brod
and read the prose of Raabe

Franz Kafka earned the right
not to have monuments made to him
not to have T-shirts
undershirts teacups
hankies undies
plates with the image of his face on the bottom
he earned the right not to
have Kafka cafés
not to have
souvenir shops

Kafka's monument stands
in Prague
it was raised without being asked

"and who were we to ask?"

the Spirit! Ladies and gentlemen,
you should ask Kafka's spirit
(and cup your ear!)

Kafka's Spirit says: please
do not praise me do not raise me
and since I'm already standing here please
do not unveil me!

I want to stay veiled

do not bring to light
my women my tears
my parents my sisters
burnt manuscripts
my wounds
do not comment on my
life death trial
do not turn this into a circus
do not draw out of me
every secret
do not pull me
into a coffee shop
do not look me in the mouth
I'm not your horse
(a beast of burden
for various charitable foundations)
don't tell me
that I loved
second-rate
actors that I was
a timid fiancé
do not turn me into
an exemplary bureaucrat
an impotent an athlete
a Zionist a vegetarian
and an admirer of
the prose of Max Brod

amen

Mr. Pongo

Christmas 2005 is fast approaching

Yesterday I went to the zoo
to wish the animals
happy holidays
I first visited the "nursery"
a small donkey
(I don't know his name)
born on September 8, 2004
is already not so small
the nanny goats were busy eating breakfast
the billy goat smelled like sharp
cheese (and resembled
medieval portraits of the devil)
the pony was sad he was plain black
and looked like a pessimist
Scottish red angus cows eyed
me with interest or perhaps surprise
sheep lounged around
in their own wool

I dropped in on the birds
they now have a larger
run—the black swans
looked like black tulips
(with ruby beaks)
very lively
gems
(though they're prone to anger)

black and white
storks quacked romantically
herons stood on one leg
beating their wings
the cormorants
pecked at something

I passed by the workers
milling about rebuilding
the historic wall of the old zoo
nowadays there are plenty of historic walls in the world

the tigers have new dwellings
now you can see them through
giant windows instead of thick bars
I wonder what is written on the white tiger's
forehead—some kind of sign—I should come here
with my friend the Sanskritist
maybe she will be able to decipher it
maybe it's a quote from Else Lasker-Schüler
A real tiger
wrote these poems
the poet has been bewitched
by a German prince from her own fairytale
stout bald doctor a specialist in
dermatology and venereal disease
awaiting the renewal of nation and race
he sobered up in time
and chose "internal emigration" in the Wehrmacht

It is cold today and the tigers have hidden
or else they're asleep—the Wrocław tigers
came from . . . Sweden; Ferdinand and Victoria
were born in the Swedish zoo—Elskilstuna.
They are "white" but have blue eyes . . .
(they're cream colored)—pretty
their nostrils are pink—eyes sky blue
good genes!—and—the pads on
their paws are pink too

a cat lay in wait for a sparrow

I headed toward
the house of the man of the forest
a house in the shape of a cage
with amenities
the man of the forest slept or pretended

to sleep orangutan Pongo
(pygmaeus)
looked at me from under his brow
perhaps he was sick and tired of visits
from excited teenyboppers
the giggles and cackling of bratty teens
children cameras tourists
questionnaires questions of denomination, roots
I turn my attention to the menu
of Mr. Pongo—wiser than us sinners—
cottage cheese boiled eggs
vegetables
white and red
Peking and savoy cabbage
(not our hunter's stew feted
by Paris Madrid London)
broccoli cauliflower tomatoes
endives peppers onions
garlic (!)
carrots beets snow peas
cucumbers sorrel spinach
fruit
gooseberries chokeberries apricots
peaches apples pears
wise Mr. Pongo!
he prefers to sleep or reflect
instead of wasting time and life
cooking guinea hen in sour
sauce a dish that calls for
one medium guinea hen
one onion three ounces of chicken broth
half a glass of dry white
wine one and a half tablespoons of butter
olive oil sour cream salt and pepper
twenty fresh basil leaves
mustard
ten baby potatoes

(serve with green beans
cooked al dente. The sauce

should be served separately, etc.)
this is the recipe of my friend Wojtek P.

and what would Mr. Pongo say to this?

Mr. Pongo turned
his back on the uninvited guests
I continued reading the menu
of our close cousin
or perhaps even uncle:
strawberries clementines
sweet and sour cherries oranges
watermelons bananas grapes
and what about baked goods?
crisp bread hard tack

finally the beverages

no vodka of any kind not even
absolut no vodka
that any mediocre
member of parliament in good standing gets crocked on
(we used to say drunk as
a sailor . . . but sailors
are hard to come by)

Mr. Pongo drinks
herbal tea mineral water
fruit compote yogurt kefir
boiled flaxseed

and what else?

Ah! boiled beef
(finally something human!)

cornflakes
honey vitamins . . .
aha! (getting warmer . . .
here we are
getting more alike) . . .

oh! these anthropoid apes
oh! these ape-oid humans
whom do we see? Good morning
Mr. Chimp Troglodyte
is delousing scratching
his head
and the one who is eating

does not forget about sunflower seeds
raspberries (!) raisins
walnuts
mango and papaya
I'm ashamed (I'm
blushing)—apes do not
blush . . . but of course . . .
yet I've noticed
that fewer and fewer people blush
not even women . . . do feminists
blush
I don't know (where? when?)

but why did I blush?
I thought of my friend
Witold . . . for the past fifteen years he's been trying
to talk me into eating apples . . .
he tried to talk me
into eating five apples
a day . . . I would eat one . . .
then one apple
every other day . . . then two
apples a month . . . then
I started eating pears
but after all I am a rational
being . . . "I think therefore I am"
I am because I think
ashamed
I hid
in the aquarium
women in church chat
or even gossip

and fish?
are silent . . . ach!
this damned erudition
belches through
my poems

finally I am behind glass
though from the other side
ugh! here it comes again something resembling
philosophical discourse or dialogue
how unsettling!

I've forgotten how much the Orangutan
likes acacia flowers
the branches of blossoming trees
grass and wild herbs
dandelions honey

there's silence in the aquarium!

the dazzling
red lionfish
looks like it's wearing wacky designer clothes
and pretending to be a fish

piranhas have a bad reputation
but behave decently
they have a subtle beauty about them
a golden gray shimmer and denticles

the tomato clown fish
fusses and fidgets

the rhodactis "elephant's ear"
fans the water majestically
the bicolored angelfish
opens its mouth

the tomato clown fish
looks like a young actor
who got honorable mention
in a singing contest

at the end of my journey
I direct my steps
to the director's office . . . I announce myself
to the secretary . . .

I enter her office
Hanna smiles
her husband has been sick
is having health problems
a limping stray dog she took in
crawls out of a basket we talk
about depression about the orphan syndrome
of the young elephant calf
about the new run
for the tigers

I hear the roar of a lion

it's feeding time
thank goodness they no longer
throw Christians to the lions
or even "atheists"

temptations

what's tempting
to an old poet?

the prospect of landing in a sandbox
with Dadaists (. . .)!
a man is a big child
a poet an even bigger child

an Old poet has the right
or even obligation to become childish
especially since children
supposedly inhabit heaven
on earth . . . Villon Jarry Arp Breton
Francis Tzara Tristan Picabia Marcel
Breton André Duchamp Vincent Ray
Man Marie Cocteau Yvan Goll
Theo Éluard are my fellow
writers bratty children
in the vale of tears
the Dadaists were enjoying themselves so much
that they didn't notice
a neatly dressed man
who sat surrounded by newspapers
deeply absorbed in them
frequented neither the Café de la Terrasse
nor the Cabaret Voltaire
lived in Zurich
at Spiegelgasse 14
immersed in Beethoven's music
he missed the birth of Dada
on February 8, 1916
at 6 in the afternoon
at the time he was busy
taking notes on
The Socialist Revolution
And the Right of Nations to Self-Determination
maybe he was writing *Der Imperialismus*

als höchstes Stadium des Kapitalismus
though Spiegelgasse
is a narrow street
the father of the October Revolution
Lenin-Ulianov and the father of Dada
Tristan Tzara never met
they did not read each other's works
they edited different newspapers
perhaps resulting in a loss
for Dadaists and Bolsheviks
these two international movements ruled out any deviations
Dada's periodical had
a different look than *Pravda*
tsatsa dada prav dada prav
Tzara and Trotsky
did not live to see worldwide
revolution Soso wrote
rhymes
and finished off all
revolutionaries and poets
using a pink bonbon box
topped with a red ribbon
even the tough Gorky swallowed
sweet bait and departed
just in the nick of . . . a bomb!

P.S.
Tussnote- und Versfüsse- Footnotes, etc.

1. the names of the Dadaists have been changed
so that the learned Dzoilos could point out
the author's ignorance and holes
in his higher education (never completed) only
those initiated into Dada will discover
interpolations introduced to
intertextual sawdust which
a conspiring senior nihilist
stuffs into his suspicious
products

2. the old poet was acquainted with
all the mysterious corners of
Parnassus he met Iamb— ˘ —
Trocheus— — ˘ Penis
Dachtylus— — ˘ ˘ too was no stranger to him
nor was the familiar sad Spondeus— — —
Choriambus— — ˘ ˘ — tried to curry favor with him
but he chose free verse
to depict the nose of his muse

3. in his old age the poet
went to Zurich on a visit
where Professor German Ritz
awaited him
and Mr. Dada and Mr. Lenin
and my old friend from Kraków
lovely eyed Roma

4. I have lost my train of thought
and will never find it
the Dadaist coffee shop in Zurich
has been boarded up
the October Revolution
turned into a museum of wax figures
charming Ms. Joanna
anounced the end of Communism
on 8/19/2005 I received a postcard
from Roma in Zurich
"I am traipsing through the streets of the old city,
sometimes climbing, sometimes descending.
It is very picturesque, a bit
like out of a fairytale. There are many bridges
and much water. The museum is fairly well stocked."
(. . .)

5. Lenin confided in Gorky
that he could listen to Sonata in F-minor
(Appassionata) every day but . . .
(etc.) Did Tristan Tzara listen
to Beethoven with equal feeling
and fervor? I don't know.

6. Professor German Ritz took a photograph
of me in front of the closed Dadaist
café and another one in front of the house
where Lenin lived, but
both pictures have been lost—just like
the professor; I wrote to him,
but he gives no sign of life.

7. the pink chocolate bonbon box
which Soso employed to poison Gorky is not
a figment of my imagination, this information
was provided to me by
Józef H. who was
a friend of King Stas Poniatowski
(he attended theater on water etc.)

8. when I read the poetry of the Dadaists
I came to the "conclusion" that:
not knowing French makes it
easier for me to understand Confucius
but my knowledge of the German language
(weakening with time)
makes it harder for me to understand why
Reich Ranicki is considered the pope
of German literature
Breton André Duchamp Vincent Ray
Man Marie Cocteau Yvan Goll
Theo Éluard are my fellow
writers bratty children
in the vale of tears

minuit definitif
accolade des coucous
progression des coucous
cacadu oxygéné
daumenhalt auf mist
reichbohne singt

Wrocław, 2004–2005

308

From

Pig in a Poke,

2008

A normal poet

sometimes I get anxious over the fact
that I am so ordinary
sometime somewhere I've written about it
I'm not worried but I am starting
to think that perhaps it is not
normal when a "poet" is not
a "phenomenon"
it's high time I craft my image as
someone wild, poetic, colorful
part schizophrenic part lover
but the problem is I love missionary style
I like taking walks
I am the husband of one wife
in accord with the dictates of the Apostle Paul

I get up at six in the morning
go to the bathroom
and so forth

I don't have a beard
or even a goatee
or curls
falling to my shoulders

for a moment I think about death
revise a poem
then dive into
life

in the evening I tear off
another page from the calendar
September 24, 2007
267th day of the year
sunrise 6:24 a.m.
sunset 6:31 p.m.
on the back of the page
is a recipe for cutlets

fry cutlets in
hot skillet (. . .)
brown on both sides
breading it first (. . .)

before falling asleep I read
a variety of art culture literary
monthlies bimonthlies
and quarterlies
and see (to my surprise)
that the poems of my fellow
poets male and female
slowly come to resemble
my poems
and my old poems
resemble
their new poems

From Jan Różewicz

Mercutio's Cards,

1998

* * *

by Jan Różewicz

You tend to come at times
we cannot talk
Father said
he was wiser
but no match for me in sorrow
I was like the lord in the Garden of Gethsemane
We are so poor
at finding time for conversation, Dad
You know and hear
I hear and know

We've lost interest . . .

From

an unpublished manuscript

2008

Mystery that Grows

to their parents
children are a mystery

a child
begotten in the arms of love
hate or indifference
is a puzzle

one they never solve
till life's end

children are a mystery
that grows with age
and then departs

Wrocław, November 2008

Notes

From *Anxiety* (*Niepokój*), 1947

Różewicz's practice of reworking, revising, and recycling his own poetic texts has drawn much critical attention. The existence of markedly different versions of the "same" poem in various editions reflects an ongoing dialogue with the reader. The translations in the present volume are based on the versions of the poems that appear in Różewicz's *Collected Works* (*Utwory zebrane: Poezja*, vol. VII–X [Wrocław: Wydawnictwo Dolnośląskie, 2005–2006]). Departures from earlier versions, where relevant, are described in these notes.

Rose
In the 1947 collection, this poem follows "Mask" ("Maska"). Różewicz's *Collected Works* opens with "Rose" ("Róża"), hence my choice here. In "Rose," a personal loss metonymically signifies the broader tragedy of the perishing of the Jews in the Holocaust (in Poland, Róża was predominantly a Jewish girl's name). In Różewicz's verse, the rose comes to be associated with poetry itself.

Mask
In the originary 1947 version, the second line of this poem appears as "where giant puppets with monstrous heads" ("gdzie olbrzymie kukły z potwornymi głowami"). In his *Collected Works* the reference to monstrous heads is absent. The second line of the third stanza, "our palates taste love," appears in the first edition as "our palates taste mincemeat" ("nasze podniebienia smakują leguminę").

heads cruel smiles sealed shut with plaster
A reference to the Nazi practice of filling the mouths of execution victims with plaster to prevent them from shouting in protest before their death (see *Nazi Conspiracy and Aggression,* United States Office of Chief of Counsel for the Prosecution of Axis Criminality, United States Department of State, United States War Department, International Military Tribunal [Washington: U.S. Government Printing Office, 1946], Supplement A, p. 238).

A Crumb
In *Anxiety* (1947) the poem begins with the couplet "She wove a small nest / out of her arms" ("Maleńkie gniazdko / uwiła z ramion"). This couplet does not appear in the *Collected Works* (*Utwory zebrane*) version of the poem.

I the fire-eater / from the conflagration . . .
The 1947 version has: "I the fire-eater / from the conflagration / in air on earth and in the sea, / want to tell her / with charred cracked lips that" ("Ja połykacz płomieni / z pożogi / w powietrzu na ziemi i na morzu / czarną spękaną wargą / chcę jej powiedzieć że").

Lament
I am twenty . . .
In the 1947 version of the poem, the following two lines appear at the end of the fourth stanza: "and with red fingers / I stroked the white breasts of women" ("i czerwonymi palcami / gładziłem białe piersi kobiet").

Double Sentence
This poem also appeared in the 2004 collection *Our Older Brother* (*Nasz starszy brat*).

I see the smile / wiped off his white face / over by the wall
A reference to Różewicz's elder brother Janusz Różewicz (1918–1944), a promising poet, who served with the Polish partisans (Home Army) during World War II before being captured and executed by the Gestapo. Różewicz assembled Janusz's poetry, prose, diaries, letters, and others' reminiscences about him, and included them in his own collected works under the title *Our Older Brother* (*Nasz starszy brat, Utwory zebrane,* vol. XII [Wrocław: Wydawnictwo Dolnośląskie, 2004]), appending to it fourteen of his own poems under the heading "Poems About My Older Brother" ("Wiersze o Starszym Bracie").

To the Dead
I don't understand Bergson
Henri-Louis Bergson (1859–1941), a French philosopher, is best known for his theories of time, humor, creativity, and evolution. On his father's side, Bergson was descended from Polish Jews from Warsaw. His grandfather, Berek, son of Samuel, had three sons, eventuating in the French surname, Bergson.

Survivor
Virtue and vice weigh the same . . .
The 1947 version of the poem contains an additional line after the semicolon: "vice rewarded virtue humiliated" ("występki nagrodzone poniżoną cnotę").

The Magician's Apprentice
bright red lips
The 1947 version has "bright red lobsters" ("jaskrawych czerwonych homarów").

living voices filled me
The 1947 version has "Living harmonies filled me" ("Napełniły mnie harmonie żywe").

forfeiting a telling silence
In the 1947 version, the silence is not telling, but golden ("utraciłem milczenie złote") and the poetic persona bestows upon himself a quatrain of epithets: "I'm a dictionary not a nightingale / I'm a poster / I'm as banal as a banana / or a pheasant on a royal table" ("jestem słownikiem nie słowikiem / jestem afiszem / jestem tak banalny jak banan / i bażant na królewskim stole").

The Living Were Dying
The 1947 version contains a number of lines that paint a much more horrific picture of conditions in the ghetto than the later version.

The walled-in living were dying . . .
For "the streets were paved" ("ulice brukowali") the 1947 version has "as if they paved the streets" ("jakby ulice brukowali").

Bodies swelled
The 1947 version has "bodies swelled horrifically" ("puchły potwornie ciała").

Salcia sold silvery apples
Salcia is a common Polish-Jewish diminutive of the name Salome.

at a gate / of sky blue
In the 1947 version two lines join this stanza to the following stanza: "and air that exploded / across a house piled high" ("i powietrza która wybuchała / nawskroś spiętrzonego domu").

with a cruel eye
The 1947 version has "with a cruel porcelain eye" ("z porcelanowym okrutnym okiem").

and apples rotted in hand
The 1947 version has "and apples rotted in dark hands" ("i jabłko gniło w dłoniach / śniadych"), followed by this quatrain: "From the smell / a pale maggot twisted out. / Apples wilted apples rotted / mother was dying" ("Z zapachu / wykręcał się biały czerw. / Jabłka więdły jabłka gniły / umierała matka").

the bodies started to fall
The 1947 version ends on the following couplet: "with chests shot through / like roses" ("z przestrzelonymi / jak róże piersiami").

Of My House
The 1947 version ends on the following pair of couplets: "On the fourth side is the wind / that passed // turning around with greater sensitivity / unquestionably points to" ("w czwartej stronie jest wiatr / który przeminął // obracając się wkoło czulszy / wskazuje nieomylnie na").

Parting
In the 1947 collection *Anxiety* (*Niepokój*), this poem was placed earlier in the collection, immediately preceding "Of My House."

smelling of reseda
Reseda, a genus of herbaceous plants with small but extremely fragrant flowers, is used in the manufacture of perfumes, including patchouli oil.

As You're Leaving
In the 1947 collection *Anxiety* (*Niepokój*), this poem was placed earlier, in the first half of the collection.

Purification
recite an ode to youth
"Ode to Youth," by the Romantic poet Adam Mickiewicz (1798–1855), is a classic of Polish literature, memorized by every schoolchild.

From *Red Glove* (*Czerwona rękawiczka*), 1948

Chestnut Tree
Republished in the 1999 collection *Mother Departs* (*Matka odchodzi*).

The Wall
Republished in the 1999 collection *Mother Departs* (*Matka odchodzi*).

Was
This poem also appeared in the 2004 collection *Our Older Brother* (*Nasz starszy brat*).

older Brother
Janusz Różewicz (1918–1944), Tadeusz Różewicz's older brother. See note to "Double Sentence."

Butcher's Booths
The Polish word "jatki" has here been rendered "butcher's booths." Historically, "jatki" were old-fashioned butcher stands where lesser cuts of meat were sold.

Rosy ideals hang
The first two lines of this poem are incorporated into a later poem, "Francis Bacon or Diego Velázquez in the dentist's chair," which is included in the present volume.

But Whoever Sees . . .
Later republished in the 1999 collection *Mother Departs* (*Matka odchodzi*).

From *Smiles: Poems from 1945–2000* (*Uśmiechy: wiersze z lat 1945–2000*)

* * * (Here is a man)
From the expanded edition of the 1955 collection *Smiles* (*Uśmiechy*), published in 2000. Therein, the poem is titled "Stuffed Activist" ("Wypychanie działacza"). Note that in *Collected Works* (*Utwory zebrane*), *Smiles* (*Uśmiechy*) is subtitled "Poems from 1945–2000" and placed before the 1950 collection *Five Poems* (*Pięć poematów*).

From *Five Poems* (*Pięć poematów*), **1950**

Pigtail
In the *Collected Works* (*Utwory zebrane*), *Five Poems* (*Pięć poematów*) is subtitled "Poems from 1948–1949" and placed after the 1955 collection *Smiles* (*Uśmiechy*). The sequence in the present volume reflects this rearrangement. Along with "Slaughter of the Boys" ("Rzeź chłopców"), "Pigtail" ("Warkoczyk") is one of two poems Różewicz explicitly links with his trip to the Auschwitz Museum. The humanizing description of human remains in this poem stands in stark contrast to that found in Różewicz's 1959 prose account titled "A Trip to the Museum" ("Wycieczka do muzeum"), in which human hair is depicted as having been reduced to a tourist attraction.

clusters the dried-out hair
The Polish verb "kłębić się," which is rendered here as "clusters," also refers to the cumulation of clouds, vapor, or smoke, perhaps subtly alluding either to poisonous gas or incinerator smoke at Auschwitz.

A Reply
The epigram is taken from the poem "Divinity" ("Das Göttliche") by Johann Wolfgang von Goethe (1749–1832). In the Polish, the epigram is cited in German: "Edel sei der Mensch, / Hilfreich und gut!"

From *Time that Goes* (*Czas który idzie*), **1951**

Return to the Forest
In the *Collected Works* (*Utwory zebrane*), the poem was published under the abbreviated title "Powrót." However in *Time that Goes* (*Czas który idzie*), the 1999 volume *Mother Departs* (*Matka odchodzi*), and in the 2004 collection *Our Older Brother* (*Nasz starszy brat*), the poem appeared under the title "Return to the Forest," hence my choice here.

From *Plains* (*Równina*), **1954**

Plains (part III)
Only part III of the poem's seven parts has been translated here as its most enduring and universal.

Down Żabia Street
Żabia Street is evocative of the poorer sections of the Jewish quarters in a number of Polish cities.

From *Silver Grain* (*Srebrny kłos*), **1955**

My Lips
taking shape
The Polish here has "taking shape" ("układające się"), which echoes the earlier line "układać wiele rzeczy" ("putting things in order"), which in turn evokes a line from the first stanza, "ułożeniem rzeczy" ("putting things away").

Love 1944
This poem also appeared in the 2004 collection *Our Older Brother* (*Nasz starszy brat*).

Old Jewish Cemetery at Lesko
One of the oldest and best-preserved cemeteries in Poland's sub-Carpathian Province, the Jewish cemetery at Lesko contains graves dating to the sixteenth century. The region near Lesko and Góry Słone (the Salt Mountains) had a large Jewish population prior to World War II. For more on the cemetery, see *Cmentarz żydowski w Lesku* by Andrzej Trzciński and Marcin Wodziński (2001).

From *An Open Poem* (*Poemat otwarty*), **1956**

An Open Poem
The present translation contains four poems excerpted from the fourteen-poem cycle also titled "An Open Poem."

Posthumous Exoneration
The Polish title is "Rehabilitacja pośmiertna." During the "thaw" following the death of Stalin in 1953, Communist party reformers attempted to "correct" the past in a grotesque practice known as "rehabilitacja" (rehabilitation or exoneration), in which those convicted in show trials and executed were exonerated and had their status restored. The literary thaw in Poland, conventionally thought to have begun with the 1955 publication of Adam Ważyk's *Poems for Adults*, was marked by a partial loosening of literary censorship. Many poems were written on this theme in this period. A poetic treatment of the rehabilitation of Hungarian communist Laszlo Rajek may be found in Wisława Szymborska's "Funeral" ("Pogrzeb") in the 1957 volume *Calling Out to Yeti* (*Wołanie do Yeti*).

From *Forms* (*Formy*), **1958**

Forms
frightened by fire
The version in the 1958 collection has: "frightened by fire and the smell of blood."

meat still breathing (. . .) seep / out
These lines resurface in "Francis Bacon or Diego Velázquez in the dentist's chair," included in the present collection.

I Lack Courage
A bespectacled critic smiles
In the original version of the poem, the second stanza reads: "A fatso in glasses smiles / you know that everyone has difficulty / explaining some difficulties / connected with that" (Grubasek w okularych uśmiecha się / wiecie że trudno każdemu / wyjaśnić pewne trudności / z tym związane).

The Tower
had lips and precious eyes
The Polish has "which had lips and precious eyes in its head" ("które miało usta i drogocenne oczy w głowie"). For lack of a comparable English idiom the head was lost.

From *Green Rose* (*Zielona róża*), 1961

Green Rose
". . . she embroidered the rose petals in green"
A line from the poem "Konrad Wallenrod" by Adam Mickiewicz. The line is spoken by Kiejstut in reference to his love-struck daughter Aldona, who confuses the colors of the petals and leaves she embroiders. For more on Mickiewicz see notes to "Purification," "They Came to See a Poet," and "gray area."

hence no one ever dies
I chose this rendering over the more literal "so everyone lives forever" ("więc wszyscy żyją wiecznie").

In the Light of Day
mouths / swarming with fake teeth
In the 1961 version the teeth are white ("białe"), not fake.

laughter flows
It is blood not laughter that flows from the bodies on the screen in the 1961 version.

a real woman
"Genuine woman" ("prawdziwa kobieta") of the 1961 version becomes "realna kobieta," or "realistic woman," in Różewicz's *Collected Works*. Also, the 1961 version ends with a stanza omitted in the *Collected Works*, which is hence omitted here.

From *Nothing in Prospero's Robes* (*Nic w płaszczu Prospera*), 1963

Nothing in Prospero's Robes
Nothing in Prospero's Robes
In Shakespeare's *The Tempest*, Prospero is referred to as wearing "magic robes" in act 5, scene 1. In act 1, scene 2, he is attired in a "magic garment" or "robe." Here "robes" was chosen to render the Polish word "płaszcz," which in turn is a standard Polish translation for Prospero's attire.

Caliban the slave
In *The Tempest*, the savage Caliban is taught to speak under the tutelage of his master Prospero, the learned magician and poet. Caliban wields this ability against his master in a failed attempt to overthrow him.

From *Third Face* (*Twarz trzecia*), 1968

From a Biographical Note
In the original collection, an additional stanza followed the line "1921 Radomsko": "forty four / this is a magic number / in my country" ("czterdzieści cztery / to magiczna cyfra / w mojej Ojczyźnie"), a reference to a passage in Mickiewicz's drama *The Fore-fathers* (*Dziady*), whose interpretation has fueled much scholarly debate. This is per-

haps the most oft-interpreted passage in all of Polish literature. Its humor hinges on Różewicz having been forty-four in 1965, hence the abridgement in later versions.

* * * (**At dawn the light**)
Republished in the 1999 collection *Mother Departs* (*Matka odchodzi*).

Notes Toward a Contemporary Love Poem
breasts belly thighs of Cybele
Originally the Phrygian goddess of Mother Earth, Cybele was an object of worship in Anatolia beginning in the Neolithic period.

the mirror
In the version appearing in *Third Face* (*Twarz trzecia*), this line reads "the mirrored surface of water" ("w lustro wody").

Dialogue
From the 1968 collection *Third Face* (*Twarz trzecia*). The version of the poem appearing in Różewicz's *Collected Works* has very different line breaks from the version published in 1968. In some cases, what appears to be an innocuous decision is laden with political overtones. In the second stanza there are hints of a guardedness about the political risks of speaking freely.

Shakespeare / Stalin fear
In the 1968 version, that Shakespeare and Stalin share a line neutralizes the presence of "fear" in the following line. In the post-Soviet version from Różewicz's *Collected Works* (and translated here), Shakespeare gets his own line, and "Stalin" occupies his rightful place alongside "fear."

the wind blew our words away
Instead of "words" the 1968 version has "light words" ("lekkie slowa") here.

the sun was setting
In the 1968 version, this stanza reads "Shakespeare the sun / was setting in red / flooding with blood / the water the air the earth" ("Szekspir słońce / zachodził czerwono / zalał krwią / wodę powietrze ziemię"). Thus, originally there was a parallel between the opening lines of the third and fourth stanzas: "Shakespeare the sun" and "Shakespeare the sea." Note also the change from "the air" ("powietrze") to "the sky" ("niebo") in the concluding line of this stanza.

asked in the voice of "poor Tom" / about the taste of dung / the salad of bay leaves
In *King Lear*, the Earl of Gloucester is tricked by his illegitimate son Edmund into believing that Edgar, the Earl's legitimate son, plans to kill him. The loyal Edgar flees the household and disguises himself as Poor Tom in order to remain nearby and protect his father. Compare the following lines from Edgar in act 3, scene 4 of *King Lear*: "Poor Tom, that eats the swimming frog, the toad, the tadpole, the wall-newt, and the water; that in the fury of his heart, when the foul fiend rages, eats cow-dung for sallets . . . " (N.B., "sallet" was an Elizabethan spelling for "salad").

Non-Stop Show
Do . . . you . . . Dubonnet . . .
In the version of the poem appearing in *Third Face* as well as in the *Collected Works* these lines appear in German: *Dubo . . . Dubon . . . Dubonnet . . . Jeder Schluck / ist Beruhigung und Genuß . . . jeder Schluck / erfrischt Sie und tut Ihren angespannten / Nerven gut. Den Tag beschließen Den / Abend gewinnen.* The *Third Face* version differs in only one line: "*Du . . . Dubon . . . Dubonnet.*" Dubonnet refers to a wine-based aperitif, with a long history of advertisements aimed at cultivated ladies and gentlemen. Here I have tried to translate these lines into the language of advertising copy.

Das Spiel mit den Möglichkeiten
German for "Game of chance."

of the group: Hoyland Plumb Turnbull and Stroud
The Polish misidentifies two of these four British painters—John Hoyland (1934–), John Plumb (1927–2008), William Turnbull (1922–), and Peter Stroud (1921–)—as Furbull and Strond, perhaps the product of a printer's error.

Never Let Go West Side Story Lolita
Never Let Go, a 1960 British film starring Peter Sellers, cast against type as a ruthless gangster, was shown in Poland under the title *Garage of Death* (*Garaż śmierci*).

Munich München (. . .) In Munich
The nonstop show runs the gamut from high art (Alte Pinakothek with its impressive art collection), through entertainment (opera, jazz venues, comedy clubs, cabarets, and striptease joints), eating and drinking establishments (restaurants, bars, beer halls, and cheap fast-food places) to tourist attractions (chillingly including Feldherrnhalle, the "spiritual" center of Nazism). Advertising slogans intended to lure consumers to local and exotic attractions are cited in a mixture of languages. I have translated the German where warranted, noting those passages herein. Except for proper nouns, wherever the German has been retained, English translations are furnished.

Haremsfrauen
German for "Harem women."

Bongo Bar (. . .) Moulin Rouge (. . .) Lola Montez Bar
These were important Munich jazz venues during the postwar period, featuring such acts as Ella Fitzgerald and Dizzy Gillespie. Bongo Bar, according to the 1961 *Fielding's Travel Guide to Europe* had a "tropical never-never land atmosphere." Moulin Rouge was also a striptease club. Lola Montez Bar was named for the pseudonym of the Irish dancer who married King Ludwig of Bavaria. Montez was infamous for wielding her influence to advance progressive causes.

Tai-Tung Beste Koche aus Chungking
According to a 1956 Baedeker, Tai-Tung was a Chinese restaurant at the corner of Amalienstraße and Theresienstraße, apparently boasting the "best cooks from Chungking."

Schaschlik Bockwurst Riesenwurst
These are the names of three Munich street foods. "Schaschlik" is a type of kebab. "Bockwurst" is a thick frankfurter. "Riesenwurst" is a giant sausage.

Bomben Varieteprogramm
German for "bombshells" and "vaudeville program."

Die Zwiebel
The name of a Munich cabaret theater, known for its political satire, that flourished in the postwar period. The name translates as "The Onion."

Pique Dame
A Tchaikovsky opera adapted from Pushkin's "Queen of Spades."

Nuremburg Bratwurstglöckl Restaurant
The German here is: "Gaststätte Nürnberger Bratwurstglöckl."

Weiß- und Bratwürste Hühner-Gustl / Schweinwürstl
Weißwürste are sausages made from veal, traditionally devoured at the end of an eve-

ning of drinking. Bratwurst is a grilled sausage. Hühner-Gustl, meaning chicken delight, is the name of a restaurant. Schweinwürstl is a pork sausage.

Stachelschweine Schwabing
Stachelschweine (The Porcupine) was a Berlin cabaret troupe that staged tour performances in Munich during the period in which this poem was written. Schwabing is the name of the university district in Munich which a 1959 *New York Times* article referred to as "the Greenwich Village of Munich."

Alte Pinakothek
A Munich art museum housing one of the world's most extensive and important collections of fourteenth- through eighteenth-century European paintings, including works by Lucas Cranach the Younger, Frans Hals, Albrecht Dürer, Jacopo Tintoretto, and François Boucher.

Cranach the Younger
Lucas Cranach der Jungere (1515–1586). German Renaissance artist, known primarily for his woodcuts and paintings. His *Portrait of a Woman* and *Venus and Amor* reside in the permanent collection of Alte Pinakothek.

Frans Hals
Frans Hals (c. 1580–1666). Dutch painter. Known for his portraiture, Hals was a stylistic innovator, introducing lively, loose brushwork into Dutch painting. His *Porträt des Willem van Heythuyzen* is in the permanent collection of Alte Pinakothek.

Dürer
Albrecht Dürer (1471–1528). German painter, printmaker, and art theorist. His *Self-Portrait with Fur-Trimmed Robe, Paumgartner Altar*, and *The Four Apostles* are to be found in Alte Pinakothek's permanent collection.

Mars and Venus Surprised by Vulcan
A painting by Jacopo Tintoretto (1518–1594) in Alte Pinakothek, depicting Vulcan inspecting his wife Venus's bed while Mars hides beneath a table and tries to quiet a barking dog.

Boucher
François Boucher (1703–1770). French painter. His *Portrait of the Marquise de Pompadour* and *Reclining Girl* may be found in Alte Pinakothek.

Feldherrnhalle Bierhalle (. . .) In Munich
Hitler's infamous beer hall putsch of November 9, 1923, ended when the Bavarian police shot at the marchers at Feldherrnhalle, a memorial to German military leaders located on the Odeonsplatz. The site came to represent Nazism, and in the time of the Third Reich passersby were mandated to give the Nazi salute.

Wienerwald
A German fast-food chain serving crispy chicken à la Kentucky Fried Chicken.

Crispy Chicken
The German name for this fast food menu item, "Knuspriges Hendl," is used in the original.

authentic Munich sausage products
Różewicz gives the advertising slogan in German here: "echt Münchner Wurstwaren."

Pschorr Beer Dance Bar MADISON
Różewicz uses the German here: "Pschorr Biere Tanz Bar MADISON."

Nymphenburg Castle
The Polish text references "Schloß Nymphenburg." The Nymphenburg Castle (or Palace) was long the summer residence of Bavarian rulers and is today the home of Franz, Duke of Bavaria.

the love poems of the past favored the description of the body
Różewicz here alludes to his 1963 poem "Notes Toward a Contemporary Love Poem" found in the same collection.

I tell him about the ghost who
In *Hamlet,* King Hamlet's ghost makes four appearances, the most salient of these being in act 1, scene 5, in which the ghost reveals to Hamlet the details of King Hamlet's murder and calls on him to avenge it.

about the rat behind the arras
In act 3, scene 4 of *Hamlet* Polonius hides behind a tapestry, or arras, to eavesdrop on Hamlet's conversation with Queen Gertrude. Hamlet, who hears a noise coming from the direction of the arras, calls the intruder a rat, draws a knife, and kills Polonius through the tapestry. Hamlet's slaying of the father of his beloved Ophelia drives her mad.

about the gray-bearded prattler
Perhaps owing to Hamlet's epithet for him—"foolish prating knave"—the presently contested interpretation is that Polonius is a prattler, speaking much while saying little. This is how he was portrayed by Felix Aylmer in the 1948 film adaptation directed by Laurence Olivier.

about the desecrated nuptial bed
In *Hamlet,* Queen Gertrude marries Claudius, brother of King Hamlet, without suspecting his role in King Hamlet's death.

From *Regio* (*Regio*), 1969

Homework Assignment on the Subject of Angels
angels in heaven
The Polish "anioł w raju" signifies "angels in paradise." In Polish, "raj" refers to paradise, whereas "niebo" has a broader semantic field including heaven, the heavens, and the sky. In English "heaven" is more colloquial than "paradise," hence my choice here.

Autumnal
gnarled prickly
"Gnarled" here was chosen to translate the archaic "gręby," which means, roughly, wrinkled or rough.

July 11, 1968. Rain
A sieve of rain lengthens thickens
The Polish has "a sieve of rain grows thickens" ("sito deszczu rośnie gęstnieje"), but since neither a sieve nor rain grows, I rendered "rośnie" as "lengthens."

* * * (Will something bad happen to me?)
poet Lu You
Poet Lu You (1125–1210), considered a great Chinese patriot, dedicated his life and the bulk of his prolific poetic output to advancing the cause of achieving a unified Song dynasty. He died at the age of eighty-five, the northern Song dynasty still in the hands of the Jurchens.

From *Without a Title: Poems from 1971–1976* (*Bez tytułu: wiersze z lat 1971–1976*)

* * * (ten years ago)
The poem was later republished in the 1999 collection *Mother Departs* (*Matka odchodzi*) and again in volume XI of Różewicz's 2004 *Collected Works* (*Utwory zebrane*).

*** (the face of the motherland)
The poem first appeared in *Collected Poetry* (*Poezje zebrane*, 1971). It was later republished in the 1999 collection *Mother Departs* (*Matka odchodzi*) and again in volume XI of Różewicz's 2004 *Collected Works* (*Utwory zebrane*).

the face of the motherland
The Polish word "ojczyzna" could be translated as "motherland," "fatherland," "native land," or "homeland." Since in English, "the Fatherland" is closely associated with Germany, "native land" has Native American connotations, and "homeland" evokes the U.S. Department of Homeland Security, "motherland" was chosen here.

the motherland smiles
While the Polish verb "śmiać się" means "to laugh," "smiles" was chosen to avoid laughter's potentially sinister overtones.

From *A Traumatic Tale* (*Opowiadanie traumatyczne*), **1979**

* * * (I waded through the dream)
Later republished in the 1999 collection *Mother Departs* (*Matka odchodzi*) and again in volume XI of Różewicz's 2004 *Collected Works* (*Utwory zebrane*).

Photograph
This poem also appeared in the 1999 collection *Mother Departs* (*Matka odchodzi*) and the 2004 collection *Our Older Brother* (*Nasz starszy brat*), volume XII of Różewicz's *Collected Works* (*Utwory zebrane*).

with a view of Erbalunga
Erbalunga is a small town in northern Corsica. A reproduction of the postcard appears in the 1999 collection *Mother Departs* (*Matka odchodzi*).

in 1944 / my older brother / was murdered by the Gestapo
On Janusz Różewicz (1918–1944), see notes to the poem "Double Sentence."

The Boat
Father lived / ninety years / he died in February 1977
The poet's father, Władysław Różewicz (1885–1977) was a minor judicial official in Radomsko and Częstochowa.

From *On the Surface and Inside a Poem* (*Na powierzchni poematu i w środku*), **1983**

I Am Noman
Later republished in the 1998 collection *always a fragment. recycling* (*zawsze fragment. recycling*). The second of four poems in which Różewicz confronts the life and legacy of Ezra Pound. Throughout his long poetic career Różewicz's views on Ezra Pound have undergone a gradual evolution, from unequivocal condemnation of Pound in Part VII of the 1954 poem "Plains" ("Równina") to nonjudgmental inquiry into Pound's psychological condition, views on usury, fitness to stand trial, and poetic legacy in later poems

such as the present poem, the 2002 poem "Too Bad" ("Szkoda"), and the 2004–2005 poem "one of the Church Fathers of poetry" ("jeden z Ojców kościoła poezji").

I Am Noman
"I am noman," a quotation from Ezra Pound's Canto LXXIV, *The Cantos of Ezra Pound*, New York: New Directions, 1970, p. 426. Różewicz quotes from both the English and the German of *Die Pisaner Gesänge* (Zürich: Arche, 1956), Eva Hesse's translation of the Pisan Cantos with Pound's original text and Hesse's German translation on facing pages. Różewicz's original poem is titled "Jestem nikt" (I am nobody), a Polish translation of "Ich bin niemand," Eva Hesse's rendering of Pound's line. Wishing to avoid the hazards of translating a translation, and seeking to maintain historical accuracy, I have consulted accounts of Pound's imprisonment, and quoted from the transcript of his trial, the original text of his *Cantos*, as well as Hesse's German translation. The resulting adjustments to Różewicz's text are noted.

the dogs leap on Actaeon
Różewicz cites in English a line repeated throughout Ezra Pound's Canto IV (1919).

he was moved / to a detention center (. . .) the bars of the cage were reinforced
Indicted for treason by a grand jury in the District of Columbia on July 26, 1943, for his highly inflammatory antiwar, anti-Roosevelt, anti-usury, and anti-Semitic radio broadcasts in Italy during World War II, Pound was taken into custody and imprisoned for twenty-five days in a cage (one of ten so-called "death cells") at the Disciplinary Training Center (DTC), a U.S. Army prison outside of Pisa, Italy. The DTC was a repository for deserters, outcasts, thieves, sexual offenders, and murderers, but those assigned to the reinforced animal cages were generally those who had been sentenced to death and were awaiting transfer to Naples for their execution. Belts and laces were confiscated to prevent suicide. See "The Gorilla Cage" in *The Roots of Treason* by E. Fuller Torrey (New York: McGraw-Hill), 1984.

Ich bin Niemand / Mein Name ist Niemand
In the third and twenty-ninth stanzas, Różewicz quotes these lines in Eva Hesse's German translation, *Die Pisaner Gesänge*, p. 9. I have chosen both to retain the German and to provide Pound's original lines.

he said an anthology of lyric poetry / he found in the latrine / saved him from madness
The anthology in question is M. E. Speare's *Pocket Book of Verse: Great English and American Poems* (Pocket Books: New York, 1940). Specially printed in compliance with government standards for wartime paper conservation, its front matter bears the inscription: "Books Are Weapons In The War of Ideas." Its rear cover entreats: "Send this book to a boy in the armed forces anywhere in the U.S. . . . . Only 3c."

that from the gates of death . . .
From Pound's Canto LXXX, p. 513. Pound is clearly referring to his confinement at the DTC, but the underlying biblical allusion is to Job 38.17, the translation of which is found in Speare's *Pocket Book of Verse*: "Have the gates of death been opened unto thee? Or hast thou seen the doors of the shadow of death." See Carroll F. Terrell, *A Companion to the Cantos of Ezra Pound: Cantos 1–71,* Berkeley: University of California Press, 1993, p. 446.

Whitman liked oysters
From Pound's *Canto* LXXX: "Whitman liked oysters / at least I think it was oysters," p. 495.

I make a pact / with you Walt Whitman
From the opening quatrain of "The Pact," Ezra Pound's 1916 poem. Różewicz quotes these lines in Polish translation. I have removed Pound's punctuation and overruled his line breaks in favor of those in Różewicz's text. Pound's original lines read: "I make

a pact with you, Walt Whitman— / I have detested you long enough. / I come to you as a grown child / Who has had a pig-headed father." *Lustra of Ezra Pound, with Earlier Poems* (New York: Knopf, 1917), p. 23.

and walked back and forth (. . .) outside
These lines appear in German: "und schritt in Käfig / auf und ab / ohne einen Blick / nach draussen zu werfen."

the dance of the intellect / among words
In his 1929 essay "How to Read," Pound defines *logopoeia* as "the dance of the intellect among words." Różewicz quotes Pound in Polish translation.

"—Do any of you know Mr. Pound / —I do"
On November 16, 1945, Pound was transferred from the DTC in Italy to Washington, D.C., to stand trial for treason. When Pound's petition for bail was denied, he was ordered transferred to St. Elizabeths Hospital, a federal asylum, and on February 13, 1946, a hearing was conducted to determine Pound's fitness to stand trial. Largely based on the testimony of Winfred Overholser, chief psychiatrist at St. Elizabeths, a jury found Pound to be of unsound mind, and he was returned to St. Elizabeths, where he remained until 1958 when the charges against him were dismissed.

In lieu of back-translating Różewicz's Polish translations, wherever possible I quote from the transcript of Pound's hearing found in Julien Cornell's *The Trial of Ezra Pound: A Documented Account of the Treason Case*, New York: J. Day, 1966, "Appendix IV. Transcript of trial; transcript of hearing in the United States District Court for the District of Columbia, February 13, 1946." Quotations from the transcript of the hearing appear in italics.

"—And did what poetry you did read of his make good sense? / I think what I read was all right"
In Cornell, *The Trial of Ezra Pound*, p. 183.

"—Do you think that his delusions of grandeur and / high opinion of himself are / something particularly abnormal? / —Not in the case of a poet"
Różewicz takes poetic license with the text of the testimony here. The transcript states: "Q. In the case of a great person thinking [of] themselves as great, is that a delusion of grandeur? A. It may or it may not be. Q. And in case Mr. Pound thinks he is a great poet, would you say that is a delusion of grandeur?" In Cornell, *The Trial of Ezra Pound*, p. 208.

"—Does he understand that he is charged with treason in this court?"
In Cornell, *The Trial of Ezra Pound*, p. 182.

"—he has a feeling that he has the key / to the peace of the world / through the writings of Confucius which he translated"
In Cornell, *The Trial of Ezra Pound*, p. 157. See *Confucius: The Great Digest, The Unwobbling Pivot, The Analects*, translated with commentary by Ezra Pound (New York: New Directions, 1969).

"—Do you think he suffers from delusions of any kind? / Yes. I think that he suffers from both delusions of grandeur / and delusions of persecution / both of which are characteristic of what we call / the paranoid condition"
In Cornell, *The Trial of Ezra Pound*, p. 196.

From death row / he was moved / to "The Gorilla Cage"
See Torrey, *The Roots of Treason*, p. 1.

during the day (. . .) in the glare of the searchlights
See Torrey, *The Roots of Treason*, p. 2.

Usura usura usura
A reference to Pound's Canto XLV, the so-called "Usura Canto." Pound, who infa-mously expounded anti-usury economic ideas in the "Usura Canto," as well as in radio broadcasts and pamphlets, concludes said Canto with a nota bene: "Usury: A charge for the use of purchasing power, levied without regard to production; often without regard to the possibilities of production (Hence the failure of the Medici bank.)." *The Cantos of Ezra Pound*, pp. 229–30.

Rothschild
The surname of a famed Jewish banking and finance dynasty, also mentioned in Pound's Canto XLVI, where the evocation of the name Rothschild is embedded in a thinly veiled anti-Semitic remark. See *The Cantos of Ezra Pound*, p. 233.

Roosevelt
Franklin Delano Roosevelt (1882–1945), longest-serving American president (1933–1945). Pound was a harping critic of Roosevelt's decision to enter World War II. In addition to his radio addresses on the topic, in 1944 he published a pamphlet titled "L'America, Roosevelt e le cause della guerra presente," later published in English translation as "America, Roosevelt and the Causes of the Present War," translated from the Italian by John Drummond (London: P. Russell, 1951).

Morgenthau
Henry Morgenthau (1891–1967), the only Jewish member of FDR's cabinet, served as Secretary of the Treasury from 1934 to 1945. Pound was critical of U.S. monetary policy under Morgenthau.

would praise Hitler's massacres
Pound's poetry, radio addresses, and personal correspondence are littered with anti-Semitic remarks, though it is plausible that he was unaware of the death camps until after the war. See Tim Redman, *Ezra Pound and Italian Fascism* (Cambridge University Press, 1991), p. 5. For an opposing view, see David Bromwich, "Comment: Without Admonition." In *Politics and Poetic Value*, ed. Robert von Hallberg (University of Chicago Press, 1987), p. 324.

il miglior fabbro
"the better craftsman." From T. S. Eliot's dedication to Pound in *The Waste Land*. Eliot's appellation for Pound—*il miglior fabbro*—is itself a quote from Dante's *Purgatorio* (xxvi.117), as well as the title of chapter 2 of Ezra Pound's *The Spirit of Romance* (1910).

Elpenor, how art thou come to this dark coast?
From Canto I, *The Cantos of Ezra Pound*, p. 4. These lines are Pound's translation from Book XI of Homer's *Odyssey*. In the *Odyssey*, Elpenor, drunk, falls from the roof of Circe (the enchantress who turned Odysseus's men into swine), dies, and encounters Odysseus in Hades (which Odysseus refers to as "this dark coast"). Pound did not translate the *Odyssey* directly from the Greek, but from Andreas Divus's Latin translation.

"Chi può (. . .) e cosi la vita se ne va!"
A corrupted version of an Italian proverb, lamenting the ways of the world: "La carità! / Chi vuol non può, / Chi può non vuo', / Chi sa non fa, / Chi fa non sa, / E il mondo male va!" Różewicz has the Italian here accompanied by Polish translation.

The Poet While Writing
"The Poet While Writing" and "They Came to See a Poet" form the cornerstones to the 1983 collection *On the Surface and Inside a Poem* (*Na powierzchni poematu i w środku*).

They Came to See a Poet
See the note to "The Poet While Writing."

run-of-the-mill Gustav / turning into / run-of-the-mill Konrad
In Adam Mickiewicz's dramatic cycle *The Forefather's Eve* (*Dziady*), Gustav, a forlorn lover, undergoes a transformation into Konrad, a poet and revolutionary, who rails against God for bringing suffering upon his people. Różewicz draws on the figure of Gustav/Konrad to drive home the contrast between the grand, Romantic hero and its contemporary counterpart.

Love Toward the Ashes
Ms. Peggy / (in a "memoir devoid of tact")
In her 1946 memoir, *Out of This Century*, Peggy Guggenheim describes her thirteen-month affair with a man she refers to simply as "Oblomov," an allusion to the eponymous title character of Ivan Goncharov's 1859 novel, the quintessential superfluous man. It is not until the 1979 edition of Guggenheim's memoir that Oblomov is revealed to be her nickname for Beckett.

More Pricks Than Kicks
A collection of short prose pieces by Beckett, published in London in 1934, after having been banned by the Irish Censorship Board.

as if the fur coat of Sucky Molly / were yawning shedding fur
Sucky Molly is a character in Beckett's 1951 novel *Malone Dies*.

and instead of / Virginia Woolf's / famed "birds of Paradise"
Birds of Paradise flutter throughout Virginia Woolf's writings but alight quite conspicuously on the pages of her 1925 novel *Mrs. Dalloway*.

"sans voix parmi les voix" / "among the voices voiceless"
A line from Beckett's 1948 poem "what would I do without this world faceless incurious" ("que ferais-je sans ce monde sans visage sans questions"). Różewicz gives only the French line. The English translation, Beckett's own, appears in: Samuel Beckett, *Collected Poems in English and French* (London: John Calder, 1977), pp. 58–59.

On Felling a Tree
Jarosław Iwaszkiewicz
Jarosław Iwaszkiewicz (1894–1980), Polish Poet, novelist, playwright, and esssayist whose prose works were marked by moral anxiety.

the bark the pulp the heart
"Heart" was chosen to render the Polish "rdzeń" (core or central part).

The Poet's Return
Jan Zych
Jan Zych (1931–1995), poet and translator, is best known for his translations of Pablo Neruda, Federico García Lorca, and Gabriel García Márquez into Polish. During an international poetry seminar held in Mexico City during the 1960s, Zych served as an interpreter between, among others, Różewicz and W. S. Merwin.

hummingbird overhead
Zych's 1972 collection of poetry was titled *In Praise of the Hummingbird* (*Pochwała kolibra*).

golden Tepotzotlán
Tepotzotlán is an ancient city located seventy miles northeast of Mexico City.

Face *a volume of poetry*
Różewicz's 1966 collection *Twarz* (*Face*).

El Presidente Hotel
El Presidente Hotel, now Presidente InterContinental, is located in Mexico City's
Polanco district.

A Poem
in Park Południowy
Park Południowy (literally "South Park") in the city of Wrocław, Poland, has for years
been the site of the poet's daily walks.

From *Bas-Relief (Płaskorzeźba)*, 1991

* * * (Time hastens)
Konstanty Puzyna
Konstanty Puzyna (1929–1989) was a Polish theater critic, essayist, and poet.

"Der Tod ist ein Meister aus Deutschland"
Der Tod ist ein Meister aus Deutschland
A recurring line in Paul Celan's poem "Todesfugue," from the 1952 collection *Poppies
and Memory* (*Mohn und Gedächtnis*).

In memory of Paul Celan
Poet and translator Paul Celan (1920–1970) was born Paul Antschel to German-
speaking Jewish parents in Czernowitz, Bukovina, Romania (now Czernovtsy,
Ukraine). His parents perished in the Holocaust. Antschel survived in a forced-labor
camp, and after the war changed his name to Paul Celan. His intellectual and personal
relations with philosopher Martin Heidegger (1889–1976) are the subject of James K.
Lyon's monograph *Paul Celan & Martin Heidegger: An Unresolved Conversation,
1951–1970* (Baltimore: Johns Hopkins University Press, 2006).

"What good are poets in time of need?"
Translation of "und wozu Dichter in dürftiger Zeit?" a line from part 6 of Friedrich
Hölderlin's "Brot und Wein" ("Bread and Wine"), to which Heidegger also alludes in
his 1946 essay "Wozu Dichter?" ("What Are Poets For?" or "Why Poets?"). Różewicz
would be familiar with the essay either in the German original or in the Polish trans-
lation of Krzysztof Wolicki, found in the first Polish anthology of Heidegger's essays,
Budować, mieszkać, myśleć (*To Build, To Dwell, To Think*), ed. Krzysztof Michalski
(Warsaw: Czytelnik, 1977).

The gods deserted the world / leaving the poets behind
Allusion to "Fehl Gottes" ("the default of God," as it is sometimes rendered in English
translation), the second line of Hölderlin's "Brot und Wein." Heidegger takes up these
lines from Hölderlin in his 1946 essay "Wozu Dichter?"

we travel and live / on the road / here and there
A nearly exact quotation from Heidegger's 1951 essay "dichterisch wohnet der Mensch"
(". . . poetically man dwells . . . "), a title borrowed in turn from Hölderlin's poem "In
lieblicher Bläue" ("In Lovely Blueness").

Antschel the wandering Jew
Paul Celan (see note above).

and with the words Heidekraut / Erica Arnica
Heidekraut is German for heather. "Erica" is the name for a genus of heather, and "arnica"
is the name of a genus of herbaceous flowering plants used in the treatment of impact
wounds. Reference to arnica is made in the first line of Celan's poem "Todtnauberg."
See Paul Celan, *Poems*, ed. Michael Hamburger (New York: Persea Books, 1980), p. 241.

in der Hütte
Die Hütte refers to philosopher Martin Heidegger's hut in the Blackforest at Todtnau-berg, which served as a training camp for propagandists for the Nazis in the 1930s. When Celan gave a reading in Freiburg in July of 1966, Heidegger invited him to his hut, an encounter alluded to in Celan's poem "Todtnauberg." Heidegger was appar-ently impressed by Celan's detailed knowledge of the local botany, captured by Różewicz in the lines: "Heidekraut / Erica Arnica."

the waters of the Seine flowed on
In 1970, Celan committed suicide by drowning himself in the Seine.

I know that I shall wholly die
Perversion of *Non omnis moriar* (I shall not wholly die), a line from Horace's Ode XXX "Exegi monumentum. . . " Here I riffed on Christopher Smart's 1755 English translation.

Conversation with a Friend

Kornel Filipowicz
In the fifties and sixties, poet and writer Kornel Filipowicz (1913–1990) and Tadeusz Różewicz cowrote the screenplays for four films directed by Różewicz's younger brother Stanisław Różewicz (1924–2008).

Pacanów
A small town in the Kielce district of Poland, known to many Poles as a legendary destination for the cartoon character Koziołek Matołek, a silly goat who endures myriad misadventures.

Wisława enters
Filipowicz was the longtime companion of Nobel laureate Wisława Szymborska (b. 1923) whose poem "Cat in an Empty Apartment" centers on the void left by Filipo-wicz's death.

are silent about Katyń
In the Katyń Forest Massacre, following an order dated March 5, 1940, the Soviet People's Commissariat for Internal Affairs shot more than 21,000 Polish officers and intellectuals and buried them in mass graves, the subject of an Oscar–nominated fea-ture film, directed by Andrzej Wajda.

"you can start writing me at Lea Street"
Lea Street (Polish: *Ulica Lea*) is the name of a street in Kraków where Filipowicz lived. For decades, Filipowicz resided at the same address on Feliks Dzierżynski Street in Kraków, named for a Polish communist revolutionary who founded the Soviet secret police. Shortly before Filipowicz's death, the name of the street was restored to its original name, Lea Street, a mark of the changing political tide that followed the fall of communism.

Pig Roast
For Jerzy Nowosielski
Jerzy Nowosielski (b. 1923), painter, philosopher, and Eastern Orthodox theologian, is considered to be among the most eminent living Polish artists.

"Remember that if the devil / wants to kick somebody, he won't do it / with his horse's hoof, / but with his human foot."
A direct quotation from Stanisław Jerzy Lec (1909–1966), Polish poet and aphorist. See his *Myśli nieuczesane* (Kraków: Wydawnictwo Literackie, 1957), p. 6, translated as *Unkempt Thoughts*, trans. Jacek Galazka (New York: St. Martin's Press, 1962), p. 33.

In Politics
The Polish weekly news magazine *Polityka* began publication in 1957, following the Polish "thaw," and is the largest circulation newsweekly in Poland today.

replies Professor Zbigniew Religa
Zbigniew Religa (1938–2009), heart surgeon and politician, was a pioneer in human heart transplants in Poland, served in the Polish senate, and was Polish minister of health from 2005 to 2007.

From *always a fragment* (*zawsze fragment*), 1996

Francis Bacon or
Diego Velázquez in the dentist's chair
Reprinted in the 1998 collection *always a fragment. recycling* (*zawsze fragment. recycling*).

Francis Bacon or / Diego Velázquez in the dentist's chair
Francis Bacon (1909–1992), English painter whose *Screaming Pope* series of paintings in the early 1950s took its inspiration from the paintings of Spanish painter Diego Rodriguez de Silva y Velázquez (1599–1660).

Infantin Margarita Teresa in blauem Kleid
Infanta Margarita Teresa in a Blue Dress (1659), the last in Velázquez's series of three portraits of Margarita Teresa (1651–1673), daughter of King Philip IV of Spain and Mariana of Austria. The painting resides in the permanent collection of the Kunsthistorisches Museum, Vienna.

a baroque putto
A cherub common in religious art of the Baroque and Renaissance periods.

Man is killed just like an animal (. . .) who will never be saved
From "Survivor," published in the 1947 collection *Anxiety* (*Niepokój*).

I turned to drink for help
Asked about *Three Studies for a Crucifixion* in a 1963 BBC interview with David Sylvester (1924–2001), Bacon remarked, "I did it in about a fortnight, when I was in a bad mood of drinking, and I did it under tremendous hangovers and drink; I sometimes hardly knew what I was doing. And it's one of the only pictures that I've been able to do under drink. I think perhaps the drink helped me to be a bit freer."

yes sure we're meat
In an oft-quoted 1966 interview with David Sylvester, Bacon quipped, "Well, of course, we are meat, we are potential carcasses. If I go into a butcher's shop I always think it's surprising that I wasn't there instead of the animal."

modern art has become a game
Bacon in the 1963 interview with David Sylvester: "You see, all art has now become completely a game by which man distracts himself; and you may say it has always been like that, but now it's entirely a game. And I think that that is the way things have changed, and what is fascinating now is that it's going to become much more difficult for the artist, because he must really deepen the game to be any good at all."

the owner of Shorthand
"Krótkopis" (shorthand), a neologism and pun on the word "*długopis*" (Polish for pen), was the title of a monthly column by Różewicz's friend and translator Adam Czerniawski (b. 1934). A collection of these columns was published as *Krótkopis, 1986–1995* (Katowice: Wydawnictwo Gnome, 1998).

meat still breathing (. . .) seep / out
These lines first appeared in "Forms," the title poem of Różewicz's 1958 collection. In the Polish version of the present poem, the first four lines are given in both the Polish and in Adam Czerniawski's English translation, which reads: "the breathing meat / filled with blood / is still the food / for these perfect forms."

through The Waste Land
T. S. Eliot's 1922 poem, a landmark of high modernism.

Gioconda was immobilized / in a glass coffin
Lisa Gioconda (nee Gherardini) was the sitter for Leonardo da Vinci's *Mona Lisa*, also known as *La Gioconda*.

Zahnextraktion
German for "tooth extraction."

they also lanced abscesses boils and carbuncles
For an extensive discussion of eighteenth-century oral surgery practices, see James Anderson Taylor, *History of Dentistry: A Practical Treatise for the Use of Dental Students and Practitioners* (Philadelphia: Lea and Febiger, 1922).

a friend George Dyer (. . .) or on the toilet seat . . .
Bacon's lover George Dyer was one of his most frequent models beginning in the mid-1960s (including *Portrait of George Dyer in a Mirror*, 1968). A mysterious and elusive figure, little is known of his early life. Alleged to have spent time in borstal and prison, Dyer was uneducated, handsome, muscular, and impeccably dressed, yet psychologically fragile and given to heavy drinking. According to Bacon, the two first met in 1964 when Dyer attempted to rob Bacon's studio. Partly as payment for his work as a model, Bacon kept Dyer in suits and drinking money, and for a time the two lived together in Bacon's studio at Reece Mews. Their relationship, often turbulent, began a downward spiral in 1968, with the first of Dyer's three suicide attempts. Accompanying Bacon to Paris in 1971 for the grand opening of an exhibition of Bacon's work at the Grand Palais, Dyer was found seated on the toilet in his hotel room, dead from a drug overdose. See Lorna Healy, "George Dyer," in *Dictionary of Artists' Models,* ed. Jill Berk Jiminez and Joanna Banham (London: Taylor & Francis, 2001), pp. 178–80.

Poussin's scream in Chantilly
In *Massacre of the Innocents* by Nicolas Poussin (1594–1665), a screaming mother shields her infant son from a soldier's sword. Bacon first viewed this painting at age seventeen in the Château de Chantilly in Paris, and late in life called it, "probably the best human cry ever painted." See Michael Peppiatt, *Francis Bacon: Anatomy of an Enigma* (Boulder, CO: Westview Press, 1998), p. 33.

Bacon talked to David Sylvester
Curator, art critic, and promoter of modern art in Great Britain, Anthony David Bernard Sylvester interviewed Francis Bacon on several occasions for the BBC.

"die Applizierung" des Klistiers
The German literally translates as "'the applique' of the clyster," with a crafty play on the word "Applizieren" (application) and an archaic medical term for enema.

Andrea Della Robbia
Italian sculptor (1435–1525) known for his ceramic works.

Ritratto d'Ignota / Portrait of an unknown Woman
A relief of della Robbia's in the Museo del Bargello (Firenze).

Wondratschek
Wolf Wondratschek (b. 1943) is a German poet and prose writer, known for his liter-

ientation, particularly his formal innovations in the radio play genre. He is
as Germany's rock poet, whose poems resonate formally and thematically
d roll lyrics of the late 1960s and early 1970s.

's suddenly / tired of the teeth"
otes the German here—*Der Mund ist plötzlich / der Zähne überdrüssig*—
from Wondratschek's experimental prose piece, "Fortsetzung einer Wiese," in *Ein Bauer zeugt mit einer Bäuerin einen Bauernjungen, der unbedingt Knecht . . .* (Munich: Hanser, 1970), p. 39.

* * * (an empty room)
Reprinted in the 1998 collection *always a fragment. recycling* (*zawsze fragment. recycling*).

what would I miss
Reprinted in the 1998 collection *always a fragment. recycling* (*zawsze fragment. recycling*).

Wiesława's smile
The poet's wife, Wiesława Różewicz (nee Kozłowska). The two met when they were serving in the Polish Resistance during the German occupation. As a courier between Partisan units, Wiesława went by the handle "Filis," and served as typist for Różewicz's first, self-published, volume of poems and prose pieces, *Forest Echoes* (*Echa leśne*, 1944).

From *always a fragment. recycling* (*zawsze fragment. recycling*), **1998**

poet emeritus
This poem may be understood as part of a long and complex poetic dialogue between Czesław Miłosz and Tadeusz Różewicz, initiated by Miłosz with his 1951 poem titled "To Tadeusz Różewicz, Poet," where he hails the poet as a new Orpheus. Miłosz translated several of Różewicz's poems for the 1965 anthology *Postwar Polish Poetry*, and wrote about him, at length and largely in a polemical vein, in his 1973 *History of Polish Literature*. His remarks about Różewicz in an essay two decades later, 'Różewicz in 1996," are both more probing and more complimentary. In back-to-back poems—"Unde Malum" and "Różewicz"—in his 2000 *This*, Miłosz returns to his earlier polemic with Różewicz, exposing their philosophical differences. The neoclassicism of Miłosz stood for everything that Różewicz's poetics sought to undermine, yet despite this, the two poets maintained a grudging but abiding admiration for one another. It is in the past two decades that Różewicz comes to engage Miłosz directly in his poetry, paying homage to their shared canon. In "Myrmecology" ("Myrmekologia," *Bas-Relief*, 1991), he invokes their childhood reading, Zofia Urbanowska's *Bobo's Metamorphosis,* and in "the mystery of the poem" ("tajemnica wiersza," *the professor's knife,* 2001) a forgotten poem by Ludwik Eminowicz. In "A Light Eclipsed" ("Zaćmenie światła," *recycling,* 1998) Emmanuel Swedenborg becomes a fulcrum on which teeter philosophic differences between the two poets. Finally, Różewicz's 2006 collection *so what it's a dream* features a touching "Elegy" ("Elegia") written after the poet's death, in which Różewicz responds to Miłosz's 1951 and 2000 poems addressed to him, thus bringing their lifelong dialogue full circle. For more on the poetic engagement between the two poets see: Aleksander Fiut, "Dialog niedokończony: Miłosz i Różewicz" in *Przekraczanie Granic: O twórczości Tadeusza Różewicza,* ed. Wojciech Browarny et al. (Kraków: Universitas, 2007), pp. 336–49.

From Mouth to Mouth

its language
Różewicz avails himself of the polysemy of the Polish word "*język*," which means both "tongue" and "language."

Not that which goes into the mouth . . .
A quotation of Matthew 15:11.

In a Hotel

for Yesenin
Sergei Alexandrovich Yesenin (1895–1925), Russian lyric poet, was found hanging from the heating pipes in his room at the Hotel Angleterre in Leningrad on December 28, 1925, an apparent suicide.

recycling

The English translation of the epigram is provided by the translator. Wherever the German has been replaced by an English translation, italics have been used and the German provided in the notes.

the orchestra plays Highlander, aren't you sad
"*Góralu, czy ci nie żal*" (Highlander, aren't you sad?) is a well-known traditional Polish folk tune. *Górale,* the Highlanders, are an ethnic group in the mountainous region of Southern Poland with distinctive regional customs and dialect.

"Guess who's wearing / the pants this summer?"
The text is in German here: *Schauen wir mal, wer / in diesem Sommer die Hosen anhat?*

Cigarette-pants (. . .) and pullovers
The text is in German here: *Die Designer haben sich / viele Modelle ausgedacht: // Bleistifts-Hose, Marlene-Look, / Hippie-Feeling, Gucci-Dress / Zitronengelbe Hüft-Hose / mit Blümchenmuster / Perfekt zu bauchfreien Tops / und Pullis.*

are you a man / who would like to rendezvous on / planet woman?
The text is in German here: *welcher Mann hat Lust / mich auf meinem weiblichen / Planeten kennenzulernen?*

strong, sensual, sexy, / attractive (. . .) tennis sauna travel hiking
The text is in German here: *starke, sinnlich-erotische Schöne / akad. blond / liebst auch Du Theater / Musik Literatur Tanzen Ski / Tennis Sauna Reisen Wandern.*

Aurea prima sata est aetas (. . .)
"The first century was the golden age" (Ovid, *Metamorphoses* 1, 89).

Also In Portugal
Here Różewicz has the German "*auch* in Portugal."

das lange Gedicht
In the original Polish the phrase appears only in German. Here I have added the English translation.

"Juden raus"
German for "Jews get out."

Kazimierz Wyka
Kazimierz Wyka (1910–1975) was a leading public intellectual and literary scholar throughout the fifties, sixties, and seventies. An author of numerous scholarly books on nineteenth- and twentieth-century Polish literature including two books on Różewicz

(*Baczyński i Różewicz*, 1961, and *Różewicz parokrotnie*, 1977), he was a cofounder of the Institute of Literary Studies (IBL).

"Worst suspicion" (. . .) According to the BBC
The text is in German here: *Schlimmer Verdacht / die Schweiz hat. möglicherweise / unmittelbar nach dem 2. Weltkrieg / wissentlich Goldmünzen / aus Gold von Zahnfül-lungen / von Holocaust-Opfern geprägt (. . .) / so der britische TV-Sender BBC.*

wrote a book The Excluded Economy: Life As If
Wyka's classic 1945 study of the Nazi Occupation of Poland, "Gospodarka Wyłączona" (The Excluded Economy), published in the collection of essays, *Życie na niby* (trans-lated into English as *Life as If*), focused on Poles' day-to-day strategies for circumvent-ing Nazi rule, such as bribery, illicit trade, and feigned employment. Wyka argued that these practices were likely to wreak havoc with Polish civil society once independence was restored.

orchard owners near Wyszków held
Wyszków (Yiddish name "Vyshkava") lies northeast of Warsaw and was the site of a Jewish shtetl, population 4,500, obliterated during the German occupation.

the great sacred wood begins to move / it advances toward
An allusion to the prophecy of the Third Apparition in act 1, scene 4 of *Macbeth*: "Macbeth shall never vanquish'd be until / Great Birnam wood to high Dunsinane hill / Shall come against him."

Jewish Muslim Algerian
The Polish text has "Jewish Arab Algerian."

Raphael's Gypsy Madonna
Here the poet may have in mind Titian's *Gypsy Madonna* (ca. 1512, Kunsthistorisches Museum, Vienna).

Danger on Your Plate / Steering Clear of Steak and Roast
Translated from the German: *Gefahr auf dem Teller / Die Abkehr von Steak und Braten.*

"The farmers' union president (. . .) from Schleswig-Holstein'"
Here the text is in German: *Bauernverband-Präsident / rief die Bevölkerung auf / mit einem "Extra-Rouladentag / für gesunde Nahrung / aus Schleswig-Holstein" / zu demonstrieren.*

in the county of Hannover
Translated from the German: *in Landkreis Hannover.*

the possibility of BSE contamination cannot (. . .) have been used
Translated from the German: *nicht auszuschließen sind BSE / -Erreger auch bei Rin-derbouillon / auch Wurstwaren können / mit BSE-Erregern belastet sein / vor allem wenn Rinderhirn / verarbeitet wurde.*

Beware of imports!
Translated from the German: *also Vorsicht vor Importware!*

Mommy mommy what about our Jell-O
Gelatin, such as is found in Jell-O, is made from cow's hooves.

let there be war the world around (. . .) may peace and joy go round and round
The song comes from Stanisław Wyspiański's (1869–1907) play *The Wedding* ("Wesele").

Felix Austria
"Felix Austria" (Austria the Happy One), besides being a national slogan on a par with America the Beautiful, is also a leading Austrian brand of canned goods and catsup.

(for Austrian cooking)
Translated from the German: *für Österr. Küche.*

Beef—selling like hotcakes
Translated from the German: *Rinde hoch in Kurs.*

evidently the pathogens (. . .) are found in all living organisms
Here the text is in German: *offensichtlich sind die Auslöser / des Hirnverfalls PRIONEN / das sind degenerierte Proteine, / Eiweißmoleküle, deren gesunde Form / in Lebewesen allgegenwärtig / ist.*

now Rosie's milk (. . .) in breast milk
Here the text is in German: *darum enthält Rosies Milch / jetzt das Protien "Alpha-Lactalbumin." / ein Eiweiß das sonst nur in / Muttermilch vorkommt.*

Doctors warn (. . .) from the glands of sheep
Here the text is in German: *Ärzte warnen zudem vor / Frischzellenkuren für die / Injektionen. die häufig aus Drüsen / von Schafen gewonnen werden.*

sheep embryos and newborns have been lobotomized (. . .) of millionaires whores and gangsters
Sheep embryos are indeed used in the manufacture of skincare products such as facial masks and serums and in cosmetic injections euphemistically called "fresh cell replacement."

Many people already carry the / pathogens inside them
Translated from the German: *Viele Menschen tragen den Erreger / bereits in sich.*

Knackeries (. . .) from Creutzfeldt-Jakob disease
Translated from the German: *Die Abdeckereien / im Vereinigten Königreich / kommen mit dem Abfackeln / der Leichenberge kaum noch nach / Creutzfeldt-Jakob-Syndrom.*

Another form of CJD (. . .) grin madly in its final stages
Translated from the German: *Eine andere Form von CJS / heißt "Kuru"—der Lachende Tod. / Denn viele seiner Opfer verfallen / im Endstadium in ein irres Grinsen.* "Kuru" is a term for transmissible spongiform encephalopathy (TSE), a fatal neurological disorder, traceable to the cannibalistic practice of honoring the dead by eating them. Throughout the 1950s and 1960s, epidemics of kuru ravaged New Guinea. TSE is also hypothesized to have been a factor in the extinction of Neanderthal humans.

Great Britain plays "blinde Kuh"
"*blinde Kuh*" is German for "blind cow."

In the originary text, Różewicz appends the following postscript:
"*Recycling* consists of three parts: Part I—Fashion, Part II—Gold, Part III—Meat. Though formally Gold still has the structure of a long poem, Fashion and Meat fall within the genre of 'virtual poetry.' Part III—Meat, assumes the form of a garbage dump in which there is no center, no core. A deliberate fallowness and inescapability became the main building blocks of this work . . . the Madness of CJD-infected humans originates in the mad brain of an animal. BSE turns against human beings. The criminal amorality of science combines with politics, economics and the stock market. It all comes full circle . . . neither conscience nor common sense offers any guarantee that humans will not one day be mass-producing human bodies and animal forms devoid

of a so-called soul. Anything can fit into the human brain: prions, quanta, gods and demons. . . . The question of philosophers and ordinary people, *unde malum?*—where does evil come from?—finds a very pessimistic answer, and one unpleasant for mankind."

From *the professor's knife (nożyk profesora)*, **2001**

the professor's knife
to a Norwid poem
This scene mirrors one depicted in "The Past" by Polish poet Cyprian Norwid (1821–1883).

"The past is today (. . .) Where no one has ever been"
Here Różewicz quotes in full the last stanza of "The Past." For an alternative translation see Cyprian Norwid, *Poems, Letters, Drawings* (Manchester, UK: Carcanet, 2000), p. 48.

loaded with banal Evil
A reference to the principal argument in Hannah Arendt's "On the Banality of Evil."

like blackbirds (. . .) no singing rises
An allusion to the old English nursery rhyme "Sing a Song of Sixpence": ". . . Four and twenty blackbirds, / baked in a pie. / When the pie was opened, / the birds began to sing." Apparently this refers to a sixteenth-century recipe for a pie containing live birds, such that when the pie was served the birds would fly out and create an amusing diversion among the guests.

becomes / a monument
The *Cattle Car—Memorial to the Deportees* (Moshe Safdie, wood and metal, 1995) at Yad Vashem in Jerusalem consists of a cattle car, perched at the end of a severed track, suspended above an abyss. Jan Stolarczyk's photograph of the memorial graces the back cover of Różewicz's 2001 collection *the professor's knife* [*nożyk profesora*].

after all these years I'm sitting with Mieczysław
Mieczysław Porębski (b. 1921), a professor of art history at Jagiellonian University in Kraków and major theoretician of avant-garde art, was a prisoner in the Groß-Rosen and Sachsenhausen concentration camps. His autobiographical novel is titled *Ż*.

that was probably a Wańkowicz slogan
Melchior Wańkowicz (1892–1974), Polish writer, author of the trilogy *Following in Columbus' Footsteps* (*W ślady Kolumba*), 1967–1969. His slogan, "Sugar Makes You Strong," contributed to the success of the Polish beet sugar industry during the interwar period.

from Warsaw to Częstochowa
Częstochowa, Poland, is the destination of an annual Catholic pilgrimage paying homage to the Black Madonna.

inside everyone there lurks a heroic monk Robak / Jankiel or Konrad Wallenrod
Robak and Jankiel are protagonists of the Polish epic novel in verse, *Pan Tadeusz*, by Adam Mickiewicz. Robak, a mysterious monk, serves the patriotic cause as he repents for the misdeeds of his youth. Jankiel, a musically gifted Jew, is an exemplary Polish patriot. Konrad Wallenrod, title hero of Adam Mickiewicz's historical novel in verse, is a classic example of a subversive patriot: Lithuanian by birth, Wallenrod rises through the order of the Teutonic knights and becomes their Grand Master only to

lead them on a disastrous expedition, which leads to their demise. For other references to Mickiewicz see notes to "Purification," "Green Rose," "They Came to See a Poet," and "Alarm Clock."

I need to look it up in Kopaliński
Władysław Kopaliński (1907–2007) was a renowned Polish lexicographer whose many dictionaries made his name a household word on a par with the American lexicographer Noah Webster. Most likely the reference here is to Kopaliński's *Dictionary of Myths and Cultural Traditions.*

at the Matejko exhibit in Paris
Jan Matejko (1838–1893), Polish painter known for his paintings of historical subjects, often patriotic in content.

Art is like a banner on the tower of human works
A nearly exact quotation from Norwid's *Promethidion* (Paris 1851), a book-length poem on art, written in the form of a dialogue.

Hania's grave
Anna (Hania) Porębska, the wife of Mieczysław Porębski, was an art historian and a translator from the German.

to the grave of Przyboś's wife Bronia
See note to Julian Przyboś below.

Kochanowski's thing
Jan Kochanowski (1530–1584), a giant of Polish Renaissance poetry, credited with transforming the Polish language. He often wrote beneath a linden tree, the subject of one of his best-known poems.

it lay amidst Matejko and Rodakowski / Kantor Jaremianka and Stern
Henryk Rodakowski (1823–1894), painter known for his portraits and allegorical scenes. Tadeusz Kantor (1915–1990), theater director, set designer, painter, known for his revolutionary theatrical productions; played a crucial role in unifying the Kraków artistic community. Maria Jarema (aka Jaremianka, 1908–1958) major avant-garde painter, sculptor, and set designer; studied under Xawery Dunikowski. Together with Kantor, Jarema founded the legendary Cricot 2 Theater. Jonasz Stern (1904–1988), painter known for his abstract paintings, collages, and mixed media. In 1943, during the liquidation of the Lwów ghetto, he faced execution by firing squad, feigned his own death, and escaped.

Alina Szapocznikow (. . .) and Nowosielski amidst
Alina Szapocznikow (1926–1973), sculptor particularly noted for her small-scale sculptures where her delicate style and sensitivity to materials expressed itself; created her own vocabulary of form for reflecting the changes that happen in the human body. During World War II, she was a prisoner in concentration camps at Auschwitz, Bergen-Belsen, and Teresin. Tadeusz Brzozowski (1918-1987), painter whose works were simultaneously representational and abstract. He also acted in Kantor's underground theater. On Nowosielski see note to "Pig Roast." Two poems in the present collection— "Pig Roast" and "Stick on Water"—are dedicated to Nowosielski.

the March of "writers go write!"
First part of an anti-Semitic slogan, completed by "Zionists go to Zion." The "anti-Zionist" aspect of a much wider 1968 Communist assault (under Premier Władysław Gomułka) on dissident intellectuals and students drove close to twenty thousand Jews and people of Jewish origin to leave Poland.

the next day I ran into / Przyboś in Zachęta
Julian Przyboś (1901–1970), Polish avant-garde poet. Zachęta: a society set up in 1860 in Warsaw to promote Polish art after Poland lost its independence. Since 1900 it has had its own building, still used for prominent exhibits and other cultural events.

Strumiłło Nowosielski Brzozowski
Andrzej Strumiłło (b. 1928), painter, graphic artist, photographer, and curator for the Ethnographic Museum in Kraków.

Blind tracks
In railroad terminology, these are dead-end spurs.

leaving the army
Military service is mandatory in Poland.

that's Alina, I think to myself
A reference to Alina Szapocznikow.

the student of Xawery Dunikowski
Xawery Dunikowski (1875–1964), sculptor who severed ties with academic conventions. His works gave voice to the subjective expressions and existential anxiety of the artist. He was imprisoned at Auschwitz from 1940 until the end of World War II.

I am a Satyr (. . .) "tall trees"
Różewicz served with the Polish Partisans during World War II under the name "Satyr." "Tall trees" was the code name for the place where his unit was stationed.

and something even more cruel than iron—gold . . .
This is a translation of an excerpt from Anna Kaminska's liberal translation of Ovid's *Metamorphoses*, Book I.

I came to Ustroń again
Mieczysław Porębski splits his residence between Warsaw and Ustroń on the Baltic Sea.

I wanted to see the hometown of the poet Jawień
Jawień was one of the pen names of Karol Wojtyła (1920–2005), who became John Paul II. Not only a poet and pope, Wojtyła, of the same generation as Różewicz and Porębski, was part of the theater scene during World War II.

Ghost Ship
Ghost Ship
German Expressionist poet Gottfried Benn (1886–1956), was a physician by training with specializations in venereology and dermatology. From 1912 to 1913 Benn performed hundreds of autopsies at Westend Hospital in Berlin. Emotionally exhausted, he took a job as a ship's physician in order to recuperate—hence references to the ship as sanitarium (a convalescent home). Suffering from seasickness, he disembarked in New York. The ship he was to have served on subsequently sank without survivors on its return passage to Europe.

around woman's dark places
Różewicz quotes a line from Benn's poem "Bar" in the original German: "*um die dunklen Stellen der Frau.*" The poem comes from Benn's 1953 collection *Destillationen*.

stick on water
The original title of the poem is "patyczek" ("a little twig"), evocative of the saying "patykiem po wodzie pisane" (written with a twig on water), originally a Buddhist metaphor for impermanence, developed in the *Udanavarga*. This poem did not appear in the original version of *the professor's knife*. It was added to the collection in the version published in the *Collected Works*.

A Kraków poem for Zosia and Jerzy Nowosielski
Różewicz's friendship with the painter Jerzy Nowosielski dates back to the 1940s. Zofia and Jerzy Nowosielski have been major benefactors of art and culture and established a foundation in Kraków for the promotion of the arts. For more on Jerzy Nowosielski, see notes to "Pig Roast" and "the professor's knife."

("the crown of my head / became a white bird")
From Jan Kochanowski's "Song XXIV" ("Już mi w ptaka białego / wierzch się głowy mieni"), which is in turn a free translation of Horace's "Ode 2.20" : "pelles et album mutor in alitem" ("and I am changed into a white bird"). For more on Kochanowski see notes to "the professor's knife."

"Whereof one / cannot speak . . . "
In his *Tractatus Logico-Philosophicus* (1922), Wittgenstein writes: "The book deals with the problems of philosophy and shows, as I believe, that the method of formulating these problems rests on the misunderstanding of the logic of our language. Its whole meaning could be summed up somewhat as follows: What can be said at all can be said clearly; and whereof one cannot speak thereof one must be silent" (Ogden translation, p. 27). Różewicz truncates Wittgenstein's German here: "Wovon man nicht / sprechen kann . . . "

but Tadeusz Kantor is already gone (. . .) and Hania Porębska
Here Różewicz references his close friends, Kraków artists and writers who are now dead. On Kantor and Brzozowski see notes to "the professor's knife." Maria Jarema (aka Jaremianka), was a major avant-garde painter, sculptor, set designer, and the wife of Kornel Filipowicz (1913–1990), poet, screenwriter, and prose writer best known for his short stories. See "Conversation with a Friend" in this collection. Ewa Lassek-Jarocka (1928–1990) was a Kraków stage actress who acted in several of Różewicz's plays. Hania (Anna) Porębska was a minor art historian, whose husband, Mieczysław Porębski, the hero of "the professor's knife" ("nożyk profesora"; see above), wrote the definitive book on Nowosielski, which was nominated for the Nike award, a major literary prize, in 2004.

rain in Kraków
The poem alludes to a number of Kraków landmarks as well as historical and fictional personages associated with the city, each of whose cultural significance is glossed below.

falls on the Wawel dragon
Wawel dragon is a legendary beast whose statue sits atop Wawel Hill in Kraków.

on Kościuszko Mound
An earthen mound memorializing Polish general Tadeusz Kościuszko (1746–1817), who contributed greatly to the tactical successes in the American Revolutionary War. For more on Kościuszko see Alex Storozynski's *The Peasant Prince: Thaddeus Kościuszko and the Age of Revolution* (New York: St. Martin's Press), 2009.

on the Mickiewicz Monument
A bronze monument honoring Polish romantic poet Adam Mickiewicz (1798–1855) located in the Main Market of Kraków's Old Town district.

on Podkowiński's Ecstasy
Władysław Podkowiński (1866–1895), a Polish illustrator and painter whose controversial painting *Ecstasy* (*Szał uniesień*) depicts a female nude atop a large stallion rearing above an abyss. Its 1894 Warsaw exhibition ended abruptly after thirty-six days when the artist took a knife to it. The painting was restored after his death.

on Mr. Dulski
Mr. Dulski was the husband of the overbearing and hypocritical petitbourgeois matriarch at the center of Gabriela Zapolska's 1906 farce *The Morality of Mrs. Dulska*.

falls on the white Skałka
Skałka Sanctuary is a shrine to the Polish martyr St. Stanislaus.

on Marshal Piłsudski's coffin
Marshal Józef Piłsudski (1867–1935) is considered to have played a key role in the movement leading to the reestablishment of the Polish state in 1918 after over a century of partition.

on the eyes of Wyspiański
Stanisław Wyspiański, poet, playwright, painter, and architect, known for his striking blue eyes, imortalized in his self-portraits. He left his mark on Kraków architecture in the stained glass windows he designed for St. Mary's Church.

looking for The Dance of Death
The Dance of Death (unknown, ca. 1670), painting found in the Bernardine Church in Kraków.

I'm reading Norwid
Polish poet Cyprian Norwid (1821–1883). See notes to "the professor's knife," "Sobbing Superpower," and "gray area."

From *gray area* (*szara strefa*), **2002**

gray area
Wittgenstein's question is answered by Kępiński
Ludwig Wittgenstein (1889–1951) is considered by many to be the most influential analytic philosopher of the twentieth century. A member of the Austrian army during World War I, he wrote the early drafts of his *Tractatus Logico-Philosophicus* while a prisoner of war. His *Remarks on Colour* was published posthumously in 1977. Antoni Kępiński (1918–1972), psychiatric theorist and prolific author, was one of the pioneers of psychoanalysis in Poland. Himself a concentration camp survivor, he helped develop a treatment program for Auschwitz survivors.

grew only in Norwid's poetry
Arguably the greatest Polish Romantic poet, Cyprian Kamil Norwid (1821–1883) died in poverty after a lifetime of being misunderstood and overlooked. For other references to Norwid see notes to "the professor's knife," "rain in Kraków," and "Sobbing Superpower."

Mickiewicz and Słowacki
Adam Mickiewicz (1798–1855) is considered the leading poet of the Polish Romantic movement and is often pressed into service as the national poet. For other references to the poet see "Purification," "Green Rose," "They Came to See a Poet," "the professor's knife," "rain in Kraków," and "Alarm Clock." Juliusz Słowacki (1809–1849) was a poet and playwright in the Romantic Ironist tradition. Along with Norwid, these poets comprise the trinity of Polish Romantic poetry.

the artist Get
Eugeniusz "Get" Stańkiewicz (1942–) is a color-blind conceptual and graphic artist living in Wrocław. He has collaborated on a number of art projects with Różewicz, most recently at the Muzeum Narodowe in 2009. The cover of Różewicz's *exit* (2004) features a photograph of a piece from the exhibit titled "Nowosielski's Stone" ("Kamień Nowosielskiego").

Remarks on Color
The original refers to Wittgenstein's work by its German title, *Bemerkungen über die Farben*.

according to Lichtenberg only
Georg Christoph Lichtenberg (1742–1799) was a German scientist and philosopher, whose aphoristic style and philosophical outlook greatly impacted Wittgenstein.

regression into the primordial soup *(die Ursuppe)*
donuts Fat Tuesday
the Polish "tłusty czwartek" refers to Fat Thursday, a feast that always falls on the last Thursday before Lent. Traditionally the feast includes pączki, a type of jelly donut (equivalent to the German "*Berliner*"). Here I have chosen the more familiar "Fat Tuesday."

atchoo! time passes I am old and lose my glasses
A reference to Julian Tuwim's nursery rhyme, "Pan Hilary."

Józef Wittlin
Józef Wittlin (1896–1976) is known for his volume of poetry, *Hymny* (*Hymns*, 1920), and the novel *Sól ziemi* (*Salt of the Earth*, 1936). Wittlin emigrated to the United States in 1941 and lived there until his death.

dipper dipper time is ticking
Here Różewicz forges a semantic connection between a word for dipper (*wóz*) and the saying "mieć wóz i przewóz" meaning "to have to decide one way or the other."

. . .I stand before the Capitol / and do not know what I should do
A corrupted quote from Goethe's *Italian Journey*: "Am Kapitol, am Kapitol / steh ich und weiß nicht, was ich soll!" *Italian Journey* (*Italienische Reise*), Goethe's 1816 reflection on two visits to Italy (1786, 1788), was translated by W. H. Auden and Elizabeth Mayer in 1962. Różewicz provides a paraphrase: " . . . *ich stehe vorm Kapitol / und weiss nicht was ich soll!*"

Dichtung und Wahrheit
The autobiography of Johann Wolfgang von Goethe (1749–1832), *Dichtung und Wahrheit* (translated as "Poetry and Truth") was published in multiple volumes between 1811 and 1832.

tertium non datur
Latin for "there is no third way."

* * * **(And once again)**
You're right Tadeusz
Here Różewicz addresses his friend Tadeusz Konwicki (b. 1926) whose epigraph opens the poem. In the Polish, their closeness is marked by the use of the informal "you" and the diminutive "Tadzio" for Tadeusz.

"the apple tree's in bloom (. . .) / red apples it will bear"
From the Polish folk song "Koło mego ogródeczka."

Alarm Clock
back in the time of the Great Helmsman
Mao Zedong (1893–1976), Chairman of the Communist Party of the People's Republic of China from 1949 until his death in 1976.

who let a hundred flowers bloom (. . .) to compete
In his oft-quoted speech of 1956, Chairman Mao decreed: "Let a hundred flowers bloom, a hundred schools of thought compete." After encouraging open criticism of government in 1957, Mao identified "poisonous flowers," some three hundred thou-

sand intellectuals who were then silenced via mandatory self-criticism, imprisonment, or execution.

I wind it like Gerwazy
In Adam Mickiewicz's *Pan Tadeusz*, Gerwazy is a faithful servant who continues to lock doors and wind the clock even after his master's castle has been reduced to ruins.

hundert Blumen blühen
German translation of "a hundred flowers bloom."

(I bought the little red book [. . .] with a foreword by Lin Biao)
It was Mao's deputy, the celebrated military leader Lin Biao (1907–1971?), who compiled quotations from Mao into a *Little Red Book* to be distributed to all citizens of the People's Republic of China, laying the foundation for the cult of personality. Biao's preface read, "Study Chairman Mao's writings, follow his teachings and act according to his instructions." Biao is perhaps even better known for his mysterious disappearance and death in 1971 (a plane crash over Mongolia on the way to the Soviet Union), the result of a direct order from Mao, who feared a military coup d'etat. Mao's fears of Lin Biao's betrayal appear to have been unfounded.

Too Bad
"Too bad" ("Szkoda") is the third of four poems in which Różewicz confronts the life and legacy of Ezra Pound. See part VII of "Plains" ("Równina"), "I Am Noman" ("Ich bin Niemand"), and "one of the Church Fathers of poetry" ("jeden z Ojców kościoła poezji").

but also the poet from Predappio
An ironic reference to Benito Mussolini, who was born in Predappio, Veneto, Italy. Pound refers to Mussolini as Predappio in his Canto LXXIV.

(la Clara a Milano!)
An allusion to a couplet from Pound's Canto LXXIV: "Thus Ben and *la Clara a Milano* / by the heels at Milano." On April 27, 1945, Mussolini and his mistress Claretta Petacci were tried, shot, dumped in the Piazzàle Loreto in Milan, and then hung by their feet from a scaffold.

Possum
Pound's nickname for T. S. Eliot, who apparently was adept at playing dead, Possum appears in Pound's Canto LXXIV embedded in the following couplet: "yet say this to the Possum: a bang, not a whimper / with a bang, not a whimper." Pound is here alluding to a couplet from Eliot's "The Hollow Men," which ends, "This is the way the world ends / Not with a bang but a whimper."

Dante Ariosto Schiller / Klopstock Platen / Waiblinger . . .
Dante Alighieri (1265–1321), Italian Renaissance poet and author of the *Divine Comedy*. Ludovico Ariosto (1474–1533), Italian poet, whose epic *Orlando Furioso* is a classic. Friedrich Gottlieb Klopstock (1724–1803), German poet, authored the mammoth *Der Messias*. August, Count von Platen (1796–1835), was a German poet and dramatist known for the classical purity of his style. Though he was a Romantic poet himself, he opposed the unbridled flamboyance of the Romantic tradition. Wilhelm Friedrich Waiblinger (1804–1830), a German Romantic poet, who wrote a well-known account of the life of Friedrich Hölderlin, died in Italy at the age of twenty-five. Mussolini wrote literary studies of Klopstock (intended for publication in a volume to be titled *Critical Studies on German Literature* [*Studi Critici sulla Letteratura Tedesca*]), Platen ("Platen and Italy"), and was a great admirer of Schiller.

Escape of the Two Piglets
(from the death camp—the slaughterhouse)
in murky Albion the law
Albion is the ancient Greek name for the island of Great Britain.

Sobbing Superpower (Saturday, January 20, 2001)
Over the mobile plains of the sea (. . .) Doubting she will find it so
Różewicz is quoting from "To John Brown, Citizen" by Polish poet Cyprian Kamil
Norwid (1821–1883). Norwid sent the poem in a letter to America in November 1859
on the occasion of the trial of American abolitionist John Brown (1800–1859), obvi-
ously intending his poem to be a parallel address to the American nation at a tragic
turn in its history. For another translation of these lines see Cyprian Norwid, *Poems,
Letters, Drawings*, edited and translated from the Polish by Jerzy Peterkiewicz, poems
in collaboration with Christine Brooke-Rose and Burns Singer (Manchester, UK: Car-
canet, 2000), p. 33.

talking with Ryszard Kapuściński
Ryszard Kapuściński (1932–2007) is best known for his creative nonfiction and extensive
reporting on the poorest, most conflict-ridden regions of the world. Legend has it that as
the Polish Press Agency's only foreign correspondent, Kapuściński reported from fifty
countries at once. He is the author of *The Emperor, Shah of Shahs,* and *The Soccer War.*

about Franek Gil
Franciszek Gil (1917–1960), a journalist who lived with Różewicz in the mid-1940s in
the storied writers' residence at 22 Krupnicza St. in Kraków. His 1946 article "Return
from Kielce" ("Powrót z Kielc"), written in the wake of the Kielce pogrom in which
forty-two Jews were murdered, was a searching examination exposing the dispositions
and attitudes that made the pogrom possible.

kept drying her eyes Bronek
Bronisław ("Bronek") Geremek (1932–2008), Polish Minister of Foreign Affairs from
1997 to 2000. From 2004 to 2008 he served as deputy to the European Parliament.

From *exit (wyjście)*, 2004

avalanche
only the stuttering / Demosthenes (. . .) / until they drew blood
Demosthenes (384?–322 BC), Athenian orator and statesman, suffered from a speech
impediment in his youth. His ambition and determination became legendary, perhaps
best exemplified by his regimen of speaking with pebbles in his mouth to improve his
elocution.

my old Guardian Angel
angel milk the one with little wings
Angel Milk is the brand name of a nutritious shake for pregnant women.

golden thoughts against a dark background
"nothing soothes / like history"
Gogol wrote to Mikhail Aleksandrovich Maksimovich on November 9, 1833: "I have
now set to work on a history of our one and only poor Ukraine. Nothing soothes me
like history." Gogol's history of Ukraine never did materialize.

"laughter is no laughing matter"
A paraphrase of a quotation from Gogol's *Inspector General*: "Through my laughter,
which never before came to me with such force, the reader sensed profound sorrow."

a fairy tale
in Bethlehem or perhaps / some other mean city
An allusion to the Polish Christmas carol "Anioł Pasterzom Mówił" ("The Angel Told the Shepherds"), which contains the lyric: "Christ was born unto you / In Bethlehem, not too mean a city" ("Chrystus sie wam narodził / W Betlejem, nie bardzo podłym mieście").

heart rises to throat
with Przyboś I searched for / a place on earth
Julian Przyboś (1901–1970), Polish avant-garde poet. See "the professor's knife" ("nożyk profesora").

with Staff I began / rebuilding from / the smoke rising from the chimneys
Leopold Staff (1878–1957), one of the greatest poets of the Young Poland Movement, influenced by Nietzsche and Franciscan thought. In his work, Staff programmatically doubts God, in favor of placing his faith in human beings and basic human values.

with Kotarbiński / I voted "three times yes"
Tadeusz Kotarbiński (1886–1981), Polish philosopher who helped develop the theory of praxiology, the methodology of human action and conduct. "Three times yes" is a reference to the Polish People's Referendum (*Referendum Ludowe*) held June 30, 1946. The alleged purpose of the referendum was to gauge the level of popular support for various forces vying for control of Poland in the wake of World War II. The Communists, who already controlled much of the government and had the backing of both the Polish National and Soviet Red Armies, rigged the results to give the appearance of overwhelming support for Communist policies ("yes" to abolishing the Senate, to nationalizing industry, and to setting the Oder River as Poland's western boundary), despite widespread lack of support for abolition of the Senate and for nationalization of industry.

I was a student in Ingarden's / seminar
Roman Witold Ingarden (1893–1970), Polish philosopher who studied under the phenomenologist Edmund Husserl, later breaking with Husserl's transcendental idealism. Although best known in the West for his work in aesthetics, Ingarden was more fundamentally concerned with issues in ontology (theory of being) and epistemology (theory of knowledge) stemming from the realist / idealist debate.

Hume helped me / order my thoughts
British empiricist philosopher David Hume (1711–1776) is widely considered to be the most influential philosopher ever to write in English.

the referendum was rigged
See note to "with Kotarbiński / I voted 'three times yes.'"

an inscription Mane Tekel Fares
The proverbial handwriting on the wall. According to Daniel 5 (King James Version), during a feast in the palace of Belshazzar, son of Nebuchadnezzar and the last king of Babylon, a hand appeared and inscribed the words "MENE, MENE, TEKEL, UPHARSIN." Mystified and terrified, Belshazzar made the following offer: "Whosoever shall read this writing, and shew me the interpretation thereof, shall be clothed with scarlet, and have a chain of gold about his neck, and shall be the third ruler in the kingdom." After a number of soothsayers and astrologers proved unable to interpret the inscription, Daniel was summoned to the palace, whereupon he offered the following interpretation, based on puns from the Aramaic: "MENE; God hath numbered thy kingdom, and finished it. TEKEL; Thou art weighed in the balances, and art found wanting. PERES; Thy kingdom is divided, and given to the Medes and Persians." Belshazzar kept his word to Daniel, cloaking him in scarlet, placing a gold chain around his neck, and proclaiming him third ruler in the kingdom. Later that night, Belshazzar was slain, and Darius the Mede took the kingdom.

eternal return . . .

in the guise of a French philosopher / of Rumanian extraction
Emil Cioran (1911–1995). His first book, *A Treatise on Decay* (*Précis de décomposition*, 1949) was translated from French into German by poet Paul Celan in 1953.

His sister "liebes Lama" / fresh back from South America
Nietzsche's pet name for his sister, Therese Elisabeth Förster-Nietzsche (1846–1935). The two were extremely close as children and in early adulthood. They grew apart as she became increasingly strident in her anti-Semitism, going so far as to join her husband Bernhard Förster in venturing to Paraguay with fourteen German families to establish a purely Aryan colony, Nueva Germania, a venture inspired by Richard Wagner's 1880 essay, "Religion and Art" in which he railed against the 1871 German emancipation of the Jews. The colony struggled on many fronts, especially financially, and mounting debts led to the suicide of her husband in 1889, the same year in which Friedrich Nietzsche suffered a mental breakdown. Elisabeth returned to Germany four years later, and became his de facto literary executor, promoting his work but distorting parts of it, especially his posthumously published collection of fragments, *The Will to Power*. It was her strong support of National Socialism that brought her to lend Friedrich Nietzsche's name to the cause. Her funeral was attended by high-ranking Nazi party officials including Hitler.

and the looks of a soldier (almost)
The parenthetical "almost" is a translation of the German "fast."

"his stomach and intestines still in good order"
Różewicz has the German "auch Magen und Unterleib in Ordnung" here.

"the eternal return"
Różewicz cites Nietzsche in German: "die ewige Wiederkunft."

it's the leaders of the Social Democratic Party
Germany's oldest political party, founded in 1863.

"yonder lies the sea / pale and glittering / it cannot speak"
A quotation from Nietzsche's *Daybreak* (Book 5, Section 423), which contains the line quoted by Różewicz in German here: "das Meer liegt bleich und glänzend da es kann nicht reden."

philosophers
"The essence of truth / is freedom"
"Das Wesen der Wahrheit / Ist die Freiheit," a quotation from a lecture by German philosopher Martin Heidegger (1889–1976). Heidegger delivered the lecture, later titled "On the Essence of Truth" (*"Vom Wesen der Wahrheit"*), in Freiburg in 1930.

"the Jumping Jack of the Nazis" / or so he was called by / Karl Jaspers / the just among philosophers
Here Różewicz quotes Karl Jaspers in German: "Hampelmann der Nazis." Jaspers (1883–1969), was an existentialist philosopher who started out as a psychologist and "converted" to philosophy in the 1920s, where he was particularly influential in epistemology, philosophy of religion, and political theory. Jaspers's philosophy reconstructs Kantian transcendentalism as a doctrine of particular experience and spontaneous freedom. Jaspers, whom Heidegger dismissed as an unimportant thinker, was removed from his professorship at the University of Heidelberg by the Nazi government in 1937 and reinstated in 1945, earning a place on a "white list" of German intellectuals untarnished by Nazi ties. After the end of World War II, Jaspers recommended to a de-Nazification committee that Heidegger be suspended from his university teaching duties.

"*This whole thing is an operetta / I will not be a hero in an operetta*"
"Das Ganze ist eine Operette / Ich will kein Held in einer Operette sein." The original
quotation has "sei" instead of "ist."

From *so what it's a dream* (*cóż z tego że we śnie*), 2006

so what it's a dream
From the 2006 collection *so what it's a dream* (*cóż z tego że we śnie*), which thus far has
appeared only as part of Różewicz's *Collected Works.*

on the shallow waters of words dreams
The alliteration of "słów" for "words" and "snów" for "dreams" is lost in the
translation.

farewell to Raskolnikov
In the poem Różewicz evokes the meeting between Marmeladov and Raskolnikov in
part 1, chapter 2 of Dostoyevsky's *Crime and Punishment.*

I wanted to be a Napoléon (. . .) but all I did was kill a louse
An allusion to Raskolnikov's confession to Sonya in part 5, chapter 4 *Crime and Pun-
ishment.* The same sentiment is expressed in his confession to his sister Dunya in part
6, chapter 7.

and started swatting with the newspaper (. . .) my name in print!
Allusion to Raskolnikov's article wherein he lays out his superman theory, according
to which there exist certain extraordinary individuals who have the right to violate
common moral laws if the fulfillment of their ideas requires it (see *Crime and Punish-
ment,* part 3, chapter 5).

the new top hat Sonya bought for him
In Dostoyevsky's *Crime and Punishment*, it is Raskolnikov's friend from his university
days, Razumikhin, who buys him a hat.

"here one must be (. . .) give you away. . ."
A modified quotation from one of Raskolnikov's internal monologues in part 7, chap-
ter 7 of *Crime and Punishment.* I consulted *Crime and Punishment,* trans. Richard
Pevear and Larissa Volokhonsky (New York: Vintage Classics), 1993, p. 5.

one of the Church Fathers of poetry
The final of Różewicz's four "Pound poems." See "Plains (part VII)," "I Am Noman,"
and "Too Bad."

this blinded Tiresias
The blind prophet of Thebes who counseled both Odysseus and Oedipus.

Krupp Zaharoff Schneider-Creusot
Alfred Krupp (1812–1887), also known as the "Cannon King," began making steel
cannons in the 1840s for the Russian, Turkish, and Prussian armies. By the late 1880s,
arms manufacture constituted over 50 percent of the total output of the firm, which
grew to have twenty thousand workers, making it the world's largest industrial com-
pany. By the time Hitler came to power in 1933, the Krupp works were the main source
of Nazi rearmament. During 1947 and 1948, Alfried Krupp, a descendant of Alfred,
was tried at Nuremburg for using slave labor (Krupp enterprises used one hundred
thousand forced laborers, 23 percent of whom were prisoners of war), sentenced to
twelve years, released in 1951, and by 1953, resumed control of the firm).
  Basil Zaharoff (1849–1936; born Basileios Zacharias), Turkish-born French arms

dealer of Greek heritage. Connected to the promotion of the automatic machine gun as early as the late 1880s.

Joseph Eugène Schneider (1805–1875), president of the Schneider-Creusot company, which dominated the French arms industry for a century. The Schneider-Creusot company also owned a major stake in the French newspaper *Le Temps*.

Eliot's Master il miglior fabbro
Italian for "a better craftsman," which was T. S. Eliot's epithet for Pound in the dedication to *The Waste Land*. In the Polish, Różewicz omits the article "*il.*"

that son of a bitch Céline / Merlin
Louis-Ferdinand Céline (1894–1961) was hailed for his innovations in twentieth-century French prose and castigated for his virulent anti-Semitism.

of the storm of steel
Ernst Jünger's memoir was titled *The Storm of Steel: From the Diary of a German Storm-Troop Officer on the Western Front*.

"There died a myriad (. . .) For a botched civilization"
From Pound's "Hugh Selwyn Mauberley" (1920). The second time this passage appears, Różewicz cites it in German translation: "Es starben Millionen / Darunter die Besten / Für eine alte Sau mit verfaulten Zähnen / Für eine verpfuschte Zivilisation."

Thyssen
Friedrich "Fritz" Thyssen (1873–1951) expelled Jews from his company but ultimately was himself expelled from the Nazi Party after emigrating to Switzerland and vocally opposing the war.

where Cocteau read / his new play
Jean Maurice Eugène Clément Cocteau (1889–1963), surrealist poet, writer, and filmmaker, collaborated with some of the greatest artists of his time: Pablo Picasso, Igor Stravinsky, and Eric Satie. Cocteau played no active part in the French Resistance, and wrote a salute to fascist artist Arno Becker. The "new play" is most likely *The Typewriter* (*La Machine à écrire*, 1941), heavily criticized by the Vichy regime.

"Midway upon the journey of our life (. . .) had been lost."
The opening lines of Dante's *Divine Comedy* in Henry Wadsworth Longfellow's translation. Różewicz cites it in Polish translation.

I was "searching for a teacher and a Master"
A quotation from Różewicz's 1947 poem "Survivor."

ei dice cose e voi dite parole
Francesco Berni (1497 or 1498–1535), Italian comic poet best known today for his assessment of Michelangelo's poetry in a capitolo addressed to the Venetian painter Fra Bastiano del Piombo, where he writes "tacete unquanco, pallide viole / e liquidi cristalli e fiere snelle: / e' dice cose e voi dite parole" (be quiet at last, pale violets / and watery crystals and lithe beasts: / he says things and you say words). See "Francesco Berni," Konrad Eisenbichler, in *Encyclopedia of Italian Literary Studies* (CRC Press, 2006), p. 187.

he descended into hell
An allusion to the Apostle's Creed, according to which Jesus descended into hell after his crucifixion but before his resurrection.

and he saw there the shadows of traitors / submerged in ice
An allusion to Canto XXXII of Dante's *Inferno*.

it was not Circe who turned a poet / into a swine / it was Clio graver in hand
In the *Odyssey*, Circe is an enchantress who turned Odysseus's men into swine. In Greek mythology, Clio is one of the nine Muses, the patron of history.

You don't do that to Kafka
Ottla's daughter Vera
Ottla was Franz Kafka's youngest sister.

the silk merchant Hermann K.
Hermann Kafka (1858–1931), the father of Franz Kafka (1883–1924).

laughed at Max Brod
The writer Max Brod (1884–1968) first met Franz Kafka in 1902, and the two remained lifelong friends. When Kafka died, Brod edited and published Kafka's unpublished manuscripts, defying Kafka's wish that he destroy them.

and read the prose of Raabe
German novelist Wilhelm Raabe (1831–1910) wrote about German middle-class life with a humor compared to that of Charles Dickens, though often punctuated by pessimism.

do not praise me do not raise me
Here the poet makes a play on the prefixes and roots of the words "ustawiać" (to erect) and "przedstawiać" (to introduce).

Mr. Pongo
First published in *Przegląd*, July 17, 2005, pp. 36–37.

Yesterday I went to the zoo / to wish the animals / happy holidays
In Poland, as in some other parts of the world, tradition has it that on Christmas Eve animals can speak.

maybe it's a quote from Else Lasker-Schüler
Else Lasker-Schüler (1869–1945) was a German poet, essayist, and graphic artist, known for her vivid imagination and inventive memory. Following divorce from her first husband in 1903 she merged life and art, dressing in extravagant Oriental garb (taking the moniker Prince Yussuf), focusing on her artisic pursuits, and taking creative license with the year of her birth, the details of her ancestry and family lore, and even certain aspects of the lives of friends. In 1912 she entered into an intimate relationship with poet and physician Gottfried Benn (see notes to "Ghost Ship"). She left Germany in 1933 in the face of Nazi brutality. She died in Jerusalem in 1945, having moved there as she reconnected with her Jewish heritage, which also found a reflection in her writing.

A real tiger / wrote these poems
Różewicz alludes to an undated letter from Else Lasker-Schüler to German publisher Kurt Wolff referring to the poetry of Gottfried Benn: "Diese Gedichte hat ein wirklicher Tiger gedichtet." In place of "gedichtet" Różewicz has "gedicht." See *Lieber gestreifter Tiger: Briefe von Else Lasker-Schüler*. Erster Band. Hg. v. Margarete Kupper (München: Kösel, 1969), p. 87.

stout bald doctor a specialist in (. . .) and chose "internal emigration" in the Wehrmacht
German poet and physician Gottfried Benn, Lasker-Schüler's friend and lover, was an early supporter of Hitler. Later suspected of being a Jew, Benn withdrew from politics and joined the army medical corps in 1935, which he referred to as an "aristocratic form of emigration." For more on Benn, see note to "Ghost Ship."

the man of the forest slept or pretended / to sleep orangutan Pongo / (pygmaeus)
Pongo pygmaeus is the Linnaean binomial for the Bornean orangutan.

women in church chat / or even gossip / and fish? / are silent . . . ach!
An allusion to a misogynistic folk saying: women and fish have no voice (kobiety i ryby głosu nie mają).

temptations
Villon . . . / . . . / . . . Éluard . . .
Różewicz creates a collage from the first, last, and even middle names of poets, writers, and visual artists associated with the Dadaist and Surrealist movements. Jacques Villon (1875–1963), pseudonym of Gaston Duchamp, French artist and eldest of the Duchamp brothers; Alfred Jarry (1873–1907), French playwright whose 1896 play *Ubu the King* (*Ubu Roi*) is widely considered to have ushered in the movement later known as Theater of the Absurd; and Hans (Jean) Arp (1886–1966), French visual artist and poet of German birth, who was one of the founding fathers of Dada in Zurich. André Breton (1896–1966), French writer, was a leading figure of the Surrealist movement. Francis (François) Marie Martinez Picabia (1897–1953), painter, writer, and major figure in the French Dadaist movement; Tristan Tzara (1896–1963), Romanian born French poet and cofounder of the Dada movement; Marcel Duchamp (1887–1968), French painter, sculptor, and writer; Man Ray (1890–1976), pseudonym of Emmanuel Radnitzky, American photographer and painter; Jean Cocteau (1889–1963), major figure in the artistic, literary, and theatrical worlds in Paris during the interwar period. Yvan Goll (1891–1950), bilingual French-German poet with close ties to French surrealism and German Expressionism. Following his flight to Switzerland to avoid military service, he associated with members of Zürich's Cabaret Voltaire, Hans Arp in particular. Founder and editor of *de Stijl*, an influential art journal, Theo van Doesburg (1883–1931) was a Dutch visual artist, architect, and Dadaist poet. Paul Éluard (1895–1952), French poet, writer and art collector, was closely tied to the Surrealist movement.

frequented neither the Café de la Terrasse / nor the Cabaret Voltaire
Both Café de la Terrasse and Cabaret Voltaire were hangouts for Dadaists and other expatriate intellectuals and artists in Zürich during World War I. It appears that Lenin did frequent at least Café de la Terrasse, where he reportedly played chess. See Hugo Ball, *Flight Out of Time: A Dada Diary*, trans. Ann Raimes, ed. John Elderfield (New York: Viking Press, 1974), p. xx.

he missed the birth of Dada / on February 8, 1916 / at 6 in the afternoon
This date comes from the quotation, attributed to the artist Jean (also known as Hans) Arp (1887–1966), a member of the Dadaist movement: "I hereby declare that Tristan Tzara invented the word Dada on February 8, 1916, at six o'clock in the afternoon; I was present with my twelve children when Tzara for the first time uttered this word which filled us with justified enthusiasm."

The Socialist Revolution / And the Right of Nations to Self-Determination
Lenin composed this article during January and February of 1916. It first appeared in the April 1916 issue of *Vorbote*.

maybe he was writing Der Imperialismus / als höchstes Stadium des Kapitalismus
V. I. Lenin's 1916 pamphlet, *Imperialism, The Highest Stage of Capitalism*, argued against the monopolistic tendencies of "free" competition that made capitalism into imperialism.

Lenin-Ulianov and the father of Dada / Tristan Tzara never met
Lenin's birth name was Vladimir Ilyich Ulianov. He later adopted the pseudonym Lenin, which stuck.

a different look than Pravda
The word "pravda" means "truth" in Russian and Polish, and Różewicz uses it here. There is a famous Russian joke that riffs on the names of two Soviet newspapers: *Pravda* (the truth) and *Izvestia* (news). The joke goes, "there is no truth in the *News* and no news in the *Truth.*"
tsatsa dada prav dada prav
Prav is Russian for "right."

Tzara and Trotsky
Leon Trotsky (1879–1940) was a key figure in the October Revolution (1917) that brought the Bolshevik party in Russia to power. After Lenin's death in 1924, Trotsky, Lenin's intellectual heir, competed with Joseph Stalin for leadership of the revolutionary state. The successful Stalin expelled Trotsky from the Communist Party in 1927, and he was exiled from the Soviet Union in 1929. Trotsky was murdered in Mexico in 1940.

revolution Soso wrote / rhymes
"Soso" was the childhood nickname of Joseph Stalin (1878–1953), born Joseph Vissarionovich Djugashvili.

even the tough Gorky swallowed / sweet bait and departed
Maxim Gorky (1868–1936), born Aleksei Maksimovich Peshkov, Russian writer hailed by Stalin as the founder of socialist realism. According to some sources, Stalin ordered Gorky poisoned. An autopsy of Gorky's corpse did show traces of poison.

so that the learned Dzoilos could point out
Dzoilos was a Greek philologist in the fourth century BC. He was, among other things, an author of mean-spirited critiques of Homer's works. The Polish word *zoil* came to stand for an unjust, ferocious critic.

where Professor German Ritz
Dr. German Ritz (born 1951) is a professor of Slavic languages at the University of Zürich specializing in Polish literature.

Józef H. who was
Józef Hen (b. 1923–) is a Polish author and playwright. He is the author of the historical novel *My Friend the King* (*Mój przyjaciel król*), centering on the life of the Polish king Stanisław Poniatowski (1732–1798).

Reich Ranicki
Writer and critic Marcel Reich-Ranicki (b. 1920) hosts the German television talk show *Literary Quartet*. Reich-Ranicki comes from a Polish rabbinical family. He survived the Warsaw Ghetto, worked as an intelligence agent in the late 1940s in London, and was part of the Communist establishment in 1950s Poland. A cult figure in Germany, his show garners a million viewers and his book, *Mein Leben* (*My Life*) has sold five hundred thousand copies.

minuit définitif (. . .) reichbohne singt
According to Różewicz this is a corrupt quotation from a Dadaist poem.

From Jan Różewicz, *Mercutio's Cards* (*Karty Merkucja*), 1998

* * * (You tend to come at times)
Written by Jan Różewicz (1953–2008), the poem appears in his collection of poetry *Karty Merkucja* (Wrocław: Wydawnictwo Dolnośląskie, 1998). Jan Różewicz was primarily a theater director who staged productions in theaters across Poland. He

directed several of his father's plays, including *Marriage Blanc* and *The Hunger Artist Departs*. His last work was *Monisz, or Satan Made in Ararat*, based on a long poem by the Yiddish writer Isaac Leib Peretz, which he directed for the Jewish Theater in Warsaw.

From an unpublished manuscript, 2008

Mystery that Grows
Written after the death of the poet's son, Jan, this poem was intended as a response to Jan's poem "You tend to come at times."

Biographical Note

Born in 1921 in the provincial town of Radomsko in southern Poland to Stefania Maria Różewicz (nee Gelbard) and Władysław Różewicz, a minor civil servant, Różewicz was the second of three sons. Of modest means, the family lived on the outskirts of town. Różewicz developed an interest in writing early on, and a yearning to see his name in print. He sought out every opportunity to publish—in religious newspapers, avant-garde journals—even founding with his brothers a homegrown handwritten literary and arts journal, *Satyr*.

At the time the war broke out in 1939, Różewicz was readying himself for vocational training in forestry. With Radomsko under Nazi occupation, he was forced to take on a series of jobs, including quality control for the broom division of a home furnishings manufacturer. In October 1942, the Nazis carried out an *Aktion* during which nearly the entire Jewish population of Radomsko, confined to a ghetto since December 1939, was deported to the Treblinka death camp (the Holocaust would become a major theme in Rozewicz's poetry). Deeply shaken by the events, in 1943 the Różewicz family moved to Częstochowa, where Tadeusz received basic training and, following in the footsteps of his older brother Janusz, joined the Polish resistance (Home Army), serving in a partisan unit under the pseudonym "Satyr," living in the woods, monitoring German radio and newspapers, writing reports and, in his down time, reading Shakespeare, Dostoyevsky, and Nietzsche. It was as Satyr that he published his first book, *Forest Echoes* (1944), a collection of poems and prose pieces. In that same year, his brother Janusz, a promising poet, was captured and killed by the Gestapo, a fact that Różewicz and his other brother Stanisław tried to hide from their mother for a number of months.

After the end of World War II Różewicz, three months shy of twenty-four years, completed his high school graduation exam. Shortly thereafter he moved to Kraków to study art history at Jagiellonian University, a course of study he never formally completed, though it spurred him to travel to museums and galleries throughout the world for the rest of his life, often to see but a single painting. In the years following the end of the war, Kraków was a cultural and intellectual crossroads. There Różewicz crossed paths with major poets and writers of his generation—Wisława Szymborska, Stanisław Lem, Jerzy Andrzejewski, Sławomir Mrożek—and formed friendships with poet and writer Kornel Filipowicz and the foremost painters of the Kraków avant-garde (Jerzy Nowosielski, Maria Jarema, Tadeusz Brzozowski, and Andrzej Wróblewski). Różewicz's sixty-year-long acquaintance with Czesław Miłosz, a half-generation older, also dates back to Kraków. There, too, he met major poets from rival poetic movements predating the war, including Konstanty Ildefons Gałczyński (1905–1953) of the Skamander group, avant-garde poet turned mentor Julian Przyboś (1901–1970), and Leopold Staff (1878–1957), a philosophically trained poet and gifted translator, whose career had spanned three generations of Polish poetry. His friendship with Staff led Różewicz to broaden his literary tastes and deepen his interest in philosophy. He also followed Staff's lead, programmatically positioning himself outside of established literary circles.

Anxiety (1947), Różewicz's first collection, ushered in a new era for Polish poetry, winning him immediate recognition. With *Anxiety* Różewicz become a spokesman for a generation that was haunted by the Holocaust, the loss of absolute cultural norms, and the failure of civilization to save humanity at a crucial juncture. Eschewing artifice and artfulness for an uncompromising immediacy, honesty, and simplicity,

Różewicz created an antipoetic poetics, minimalist, raw, and distrustful of language. Many felt that by rejecting the defining elements of poetry Różewicz became, in essence, the poet who made poetry possible again, a new Orpheus as Czesław Miłosz all but dubs him in his ode "To Tadeusz Różewicz, poet." Różewicz's second collection *Red Glove*, published in 1948, was received as the work of a major poet.

In February 1949 Różewicz married Wiesława Kozłowska, whom he had met while they both served in the partisan Home Army, and settled in the small industrial city of Gliwice, where they lived for the next nineteen years. There they had two sons, Kamil (b. 1950) and Jan (1953-2008). The Gliwice period was an extremely prolific one, perhaps because Różewicz opted out of taking a regular job to devote himself solely to writing and to maintain a measure of artistic independence. Still, he took on paid assignments, mostly reportage, as in *Postcards from Hungary* (*Kartki z Węgier*, 1953). Based on his eight-month stay in Hungary in 1950, it walks a line between a socialist realist sensibility and light satire of the documentary zeal of the Stalinist era.

A largely apolitical poet whose chief concerns were moral and aesthetic norms and values, Różewicz was difficult to pigeonhole and fell in for criticism from all sides during the 1950s and '60s. Despite growing attacks Różewicz continued to write. Most of his poetry in this period is an attempt to reconcile his wartime experiences as perpetrator and survivor with the quotidian realities of postwar society. Although he never joined the Communist Party, his *Five Poems* (1950) and *Time that Goes* (1951) contain a number of ideologically acceptable, or even pro-Stalinist poems that Różewicz later regretted but never disowned. In 1955 he accepted the State Prize for Poetry for *Plains* (1954), triggering criticism from the political opposition. In the same year he published his first prose collection, *Trees Shed Their Leaves* (*Opadły liście z drzew*). While he never quite developed into a major prose writer, he has published several other collections of prose including a volume of short stories *An Exam Interrupted* (*Przerwany egzamin*, 1960), and *A Trip to the Museum* (*Wycieczka do muzeum*, 1966).

The death of Stalin in 1953 precipitated a loosening of the tight grip of the state throughout the Soviet bloc, a thaw that reached its culmination in Poland in 1956. The Polish Ministry of Art and Culture began funding fellowships for Polish writers and poets to travel abroad. In the spring of 1957 Rozewicz spent a month on fellowship in Paris in the company of his friends from Kraków, his first trip beyond the Iron Curtain and the subject of the semiautobiographical short story "The Most Beautiful City in the World." There he met with Czesław Miłosz, by that time an émigré writer whose works had been banned in Communist Poland. Miłosz spotted in Różewicz all of the marks of a spiritual crisis, which deepened into a depression when the poet learned of the death of his friend Leopold Staff in late May, followed by the news of his own mother's illness. Różewicz spent several weeks caring for his ailing mother, who died that July. *Mother Departs*, a series of poems devoted to her, earned him the prestigious Nike prize in 2000. His literary tribute to Staff came years later in the form of an appendix to *gray area* (2002) wherein Różewicz reprints on facing pages poems from Staff's posthumous collection *Nine Muses* (*Dziewięć Muz*) and his own poetic responses to them.

Not even the publication of his *Collected Works* in recognition of his status as a major poet late in 1957 would bring him solace. Feelings of loss accompanied him to Prague, where he spent the end of the year in resonance with Kafka, a subject of several of his poems (including "You don't do that to Kafka" in the present volume) and two of his plays: The *Hunger Artist Departs* (*Odejście głodomora*, 1976) and *The Trap* (*Pułapka*, 1982). In the sixties Różewicz published two collections of poems, *Green Rose* (1961) and *Third Face* (1968).

It was in this period that Różewicz turned his gaze to theater. In his first major play, *The Card Index* (*Kartoteka*, 1968), he dispenses with the defining formal conventions of theater as programmatically as *Anxiety* had done with verse. Eschewing plot, characterization, logic, causality, and temporality, the play features anonymous characters in a dimensionless theatrical space. Opening in Warsaw in March of 1960 to widespread popular and critical puzzlement and closing after only nine performances, the play has had a lasting impact on Polish theater and came to be seen as, in the words of Poland's foremost theater critic Jan Kott, "a true national drama."

The Card Index ushered in a new era for Różewicz. Although he did publish several important volumes of poetry in the 1960s, he spent much of his Gliwice period immersed in the theater, keeping the company of young actors and honing his skills as a playwright. Many of his plays published or performed in the 1970s were written in this period. The Laocoon Group (Grupa Laokoona, 1961) took aim at the rigid and self-reinforcing genre constraints characteristic of psychological drama. In The Witnesses (Świadkowie, albo nasza mała stabilizacja, 1962), he sought to demonstrate the erosion of values wrought by a materialist and consumerist society. The Interrupted Act (Akt przerywany, 1964) was Różewicz's attempt to write a play incapable of being performed. In a series of shorter plays he mainly explored existentialist themes.

The Gliwice period was also very productive for Różewicz as a screenwriter. For his younger brother, Stanisław (1924–2008), a prominent film director who never achieved international recognition, he wrote a number of screenplays including: Three Women (Trzy kobiety, 1956), A Place on Earth (Miejsce na ziemi, 1959), Birth Certificate (Świadectwo urodzenia, 1961), A Voice from the Netherworld (Głos z tamtego swiata, 1966), Heaven and Hell (Piekło i niebo, 1966), Husband Under the Bed (Mąż pod łóżkiem, 1967), and Doors in the Wall (Drzwi w murze, 1973).

In 1968 Różewicz moved with his family to Wrocław, a cosmopolitan university town on the Oder River in Lower Silesia. This was a tumultuous year not only in Poland, but throughout Europe. Under the pretext of anti-Zionism (in the wake of the Six-Day War), Poland's Gomułka government quashed student protests and conducted an anti-Semitic campaign, resulting in some twenty thousand people losing their jobs, precipitating the last large wave of Jewish emigration from Poland. Disheartened, Różewicz left for Paris only to encounter the events of May 1968: student protests and a general strike with barricades blocking the streets, cars set ablaze, tear gas lingering in the air, and clashes between police and protesters. He returned home to a new apartment that was far from peaceful, perched as it was above a noisy tramway and situated next to a dentist's office. For the next seven years he often felt as if someone were drilling into his head.

Różewicz continued his work as a playwright, adding several major plays to his roster, including On all fours (Na czworakach, 1971) and Marriage Blanc (Białe małżeństwo, 1974), an open treatment of lesbian love and fin de siècle ménages à trois that earned the condemnation of the Polish Catholic Church, and The Trap (Pułapka, 1982), an experiment in impure form. In a period dominated by theater, what poetry he did publish appeared only in collected editions alongside poems published earlier, thus it is noteworthy that when Różewicz returned to poetry in 1983 with On the Surface and Inside a Poem, one of the signature poems of the collection, "I Am Noman" with its extended excerpts from Ezra Pound's trial and its stark stage directions recalls theater of the absurd. The imposition of martial law in December 1981 had a crushing effect on Polish culture. In polarized Poland Różewicz refused to allow his writing to be politicized, aligning himself neither with the regime nor with the resistance, for which he fell in for criticism. After 1983 he lapsed into an artistic silence that lasted until 1991. During this period he traveled extensively throughout Europe and North America.

In 1991, the silence was broken with the appearance of the verse collection Bas-Relief, followed by a burst of creativity in which he published in rapid succession eight collections of some of his best poetry, including always a fragment, (1996), always a fragment. recycling (1998), Mother Departs (1999), the professor's knife (2001), gray area

(2002), *exit* (2004), *so what it's a dream* (2006), and *Pig in a Poke* (2008). His collections from *Bas-Relief* onward exhibit a trend toward greater experimentation, with longer poems engaging contemporary issues from the perspective of a witness to the twentieth century (e.g., the title poems to the collections *recycling* and *the professor's knife*). Różewicz, as early as the 1950s, had foreseen the ecological apocalypse that is the logical consequence of the mass consumer culture he saw in the West and that many of his countrymen craved. In *recycling*, the self-described "prophet of waste" exposes the perverse ecology of the twentieth century: concentration camp gear refashioned as fashion, the madness of cows being fed the brains of mad cows, the "recycling" of Nazi gold in Swiss banks. The long poems of impure form appear side by side with shorter pieces containing reminiscences and ruminations on the place of poetry and the poet. Philosophical themes form the core of the 2004 collection *exit*. Words that have outlived their meaning give way to meaningful silences. The metaphysical void left by the exit of God and the failure of philosophers to fill it is felt in many of the poems throughout this collection.

The collapse of Communism and resultant shifts in the publishing industry spurred Różewicz to extend his experimentation beyond the form of his verse to the physical form of the book itself. Though as early as the late 1970s he had begun to feature inked-up rough drafts on the inside front and back covers, foregrounding his creative process, he would expand this practice greatly in *the professor's knife* to include his handwritten draft of the entire title poem (some twenty-five pages) with multiple generations of edits in variegated pencil hues, an invitation to the reader to trace through the stages in the poetic process. Różewicz also took artistic control over every facet of book design, designing the cover, furnishing his artwork alongside that of his grandson, and developing paratextual appendices (e.g., his poetic dialogue with Leopold Staff in *gray area*). His latest collection *Pig in a Poke*, subtitled "A work in progress," contains unfinished fragments, ideas in need of further development, and numerous artworks, including a photo of the poet's shoes—an invitation for the reader to embody the poet.